Calhoun Area WRITERS

PRESENTS

TELLING STORIES

2016

AN ANTHOLOGY FOR READERS AND WRITERS

MANY THANKS...

With great affection and gratitude, we collectively dedicate this anthology to the Harris Arts Center, its staff, and supporters. Two years ago, when we launched the Calhoun Area Writers group, the Harris Arts Center welcomed us with open arms—inviting us to meet every third Friday evening of the month in a room near their Roland Hayes Museum. The facility quickly became a gathering place for us—a home.

In an age when the arts have been eclipsed by sports and the sciences, the Harris Arts Center tirelessly promotes the arts throughout our community and celebrates not only the visual arts and performing arts, but the literary arts, as well. We applaud the fact that Ms. Molleson and the Harris Arts Center Board of Directors recognize that writing, too, is an outlet for expression—a manifestation of an individual's internal creative impulses. Writing is important, and we, as a society, must continue to support literature as an art form, and the writers who participate in the creative process.

As a token of our appreciation, we will donate a portion of the proceeds of our first anthology, *Telling Stories 2016*, to our friend—our home away from home—the Harris Arts Center.

We would also like to thank David Brown for designing our cover and Vickie McEntire who has provided many of the photographs you will see within these pages. Your unlimited talent has been a blessing.

TABLE OF CONTENTS

About our group:

We are the Calhoun Area Writers. Our group was founded in 2014 and we have seen steady growth ever since. We have found that there is so much talent in our area and our group has provided an outlet for such artists. We exist to support writers of all kinds. Our group contains published authors, seasoned writers, writer newbies, and writers in hiding. For those living in the area, the only thing our group lacks is you. Consider joining us!

About this book:

This book was not thrown together without thought. Our group's desire was to provide quality material and entertaining stories and we feel we have done just that. In addition, we wanted to encourage our fellow writers as well as writing newbies to strike out with pen in hand and share their own tales. And if you are especially inspired by one of our authors, please let us know! You can email our group at CalhounAreaWriters@gmail.com.

How to use this book:

There are three main ways to use this book.

First, read it cover to cover. We would love for you to enjoy all our stories. Sometimes venturing out into new genres helps to expand our taste.

Second, pick and choose what you like. Feel free to skim over the chapters that don't interest you and focus on your favorites. Sometimes we like what we like and we have no desire to try anything new…and that's okay.

Third, shelf sitter. We appreciate your support through the purchase of this book and expect nothing further from you. Please know that we fully accept that you may not be an avid reader like us and are happy to know that you'll have us proudly displayed on your book case (or the back of your toilet.)

MEET
OUR
WRITERS

Karli Land
CAW Founding President

Dear Reader,

My name is Karli Land and I am a wife to Richard, mother to Alana, Jenna, Jacob, and Hannah and soon to be Mimi to a sweet baby girl, Charli Gray. I am tickled pink that you have chosen to read this book. Each person whose work you will be reading in these pages is a member of a writers group that I founded in August 2014 called the Calhoun Area Writers. I can truly say that I have a special friendship with each and every person represented. They have their own flares and writing styles that has caused me to fall head-over-heels in love with the literary genius in each of them. My wish is that through their writings, you will get a glimpse of the beautiful soul behind each pen.

My writing journey officially started 3 years ago, although my love of books and words started many years before that. I had a wonderful mother and grandmother who pushed me into the world of make-believe with hundreds and hundreds of storybook tales. I quickly found a love for authors who use words to form worlds we can never physically visit but that become more alive with the turn of each page. Still today, I have a love for these artists and have made it my mission to help other writers. In addition to serving as founding president of the Calhoun Area Writers, I also lead a local critique group, am the acting president of the Dalton Area Writers Guild, teach young writers workshops, and serve on the Gordon County Friends of the Library board.

I am the author of *Baby, Don't Cry* and am in the process of publishing a Christian Devotional which will be titled *No More Middle Ground*. I speak to women's groups on various topics including Christianity in Today's Society, Keeping Self-Worth in Check, and Living the Life God Meant for You. I have also written a middle-grade Christian fiction book for girls titled *Perfectly, Imperfect*, which I hope to see in print early 2017 and enjoy writing children's stories that make my children giggle.

I would love for you to visit me on the web at www.KarliLand.com, on Facebook at www.facebook.com/KarliLandWrites or check out my author page on Amazon. You can reach me by email at karlilandwrites@gmail.com and please take a moment to follow my blog at https://TooHotToBeAGrandma.com.

With much love,
Karli

Amber Lanier Nagle
CAW Founding Member

Dear Readers,

I'm Amber Lanier Nagle, and I've been a member of the Calhoun Area Writers group since the very first meeting. I've enjoyed listening to other members and our guests talk about their projects and writing journeys, and I've learned so much from the meeting's conversations and discussions. I always leave the meetings feeling inspired and ready to tackle my own writing projects.

I've also developed strong friendships with the other writers in the group, which is invaluable. I think it is so important to find a tribe of writers, show up, participate, encourage, assist, etc.

I came to the writing world a little later in life than most folks. I was thirty-six when I first picked up my pen and started writing short essays about my family, memories, and assorted experiences. For me, writing killed two birds with one stone—it allowed me to record and share the rich history of my family in a rather whimsical way, and more importantly, I found writing to be therapeutic. Writing helped me think through issues, and afterwards, I felt lighter.

Today, my forte is writing nonfiction articles for magazines (*GEORGIA Magazine, GRIT, Points North, Chatter, Get Out, Mother Earth News*, and many more), though I still write those short, sweet essays that launched my career over a decade ago, but now they are printed in *The Advance*, a newspaper in South Georgia. I published a paperback book in 2014 titled, *Project Keepsake*, a collection of stories about the items people keep and why the items hold significance. I've also penned a couple of eBooks titled *Southern Exposure* and *Have a Seat*. I'm also the editor of four regional magazines in Northwest Georgia now—another endeavor that has allowed me to grow as a writer.

I'm slogging through my first novel, and it has been somewhat painful. However, I'm determined to finish it. I also have notes in my office for a nonfiction book I hope to publish in early 2017 and a second novel.

I invite you to visit my websites at www.AmberNagle.com and www.ProjectKeepsake.com, or connect with me on Facebook.

I look forward to meeting you all, and I encourage you to get serious about your writing today. Don't put it off any longer.

Best to you,
Amber

Paul Moses
CAW Founding Member

Dear Reader,

OK, I confess: I'm a shoplifter. Can't help it. Go ahead and lock me up. But don't think I go down to Macy's and give myself the ol five finger discount. No, I don't steal neckties and jeweled tennis brackets; my kleptomania is of the literary sort. I nick words. I pocket phrases. I carry off character names by the armload.

It's a good thing the likes of Mark Twain, P. G. Wodehouse, G. K. Chesterton and Sinclair Lewis are all gone away to that great Critique Group in the sky, or else they would surely have me arrested for robbing them blind. These writers, and so many more (both dead and alive) inspire me every time I open the cover of one of their books. When I read them, I have to write. Write and steal.

Writing without reading is like shoplifting in an empty store. (Good sentence, huh? You might want to read that again. And maybe underline it. It's a keeper.) All these wonderful books from so many talented authors are like endless store shelves full of ideas. It feels like it's all there just for me.

By trade, I'm a textile designer. I work in the custom carpet business, which is often an extremely stressful career field. The design studio is a pressure cooker some days, but two things help me get through the day with my sanity mostly intact. First, I arrive at work a couple of hours early and work on my novel while the building is still free from ringing phones and frantic sales reps. Second, I read books during lunch, on breaks and at home in the evenings. Also, I listen to novels online during the workday while plugging away designing ballroom carpet patterns for convention centers and fancy hotels. Like I said, it keeps me sane.

Right now, I'm more than two-thirds done with writing my first novel. Its prologue, Et Tu, is in this anthology. I hope you like it.

And, yes, I stole that title.

Paul Moses

Gene Magnicheri
CAW Founding Member

Dear Reader,

Writing has always been a real struggle for me. Words just did not flow effortlessly from my pen onto the page and create a brilliant work of art which all the critics would just rave. No, for me it was a burden, until I found the secret to successful writing.

My name is Gene Magnicheri. I have been a member of the Calhoun Area Writers from the start. My reason for joining the Calhoun writers group was to find the secret of writing success. What better way to do this than surround yourself by a group of talented writers whose enthusiasm and talent I was hoping would rub off on me.

I do have a lot of experience in writing, but most of my experience is in technical writing or marketing. My job as an engineer does require me to write machine manuals, work instructions and the occasional press release about new products. While this type of writing does require a certain amount of skill and expertise, this was not the adventure in writing I wanted to pursue. The type of writing that I wanted to explore was centered on my interest in journaling.

In 1996 I started journaling. At first it was just a few entries where I noted thoughts and ideas I had about the world around me and my perception of life. Writing gave me an outlet for expressing myself and offered a way of being able to work out ideas and lines of thought. It became a very valuable means of exploring the inner self and further developing my mind and heart.

The reason I started journaling was to figure out life. It was during these years which I accomplished many of the goals I had for my life. I had a great job, a beautiful family and lived in a nice home, but yet things did not seem right. There seemed to be something missing. This is what journaling revealed to me. After journaling for a number of years, I had compiled quite a collection of thoughts and ideas. One day while going back and reading my entries something really stood out. There would be an entry in 1997 which mentions a verse from the book of Proverbs. Then a few months later, there would be another entry from the book of John. Then later, another verse and another verse. What I found was God had somehow mysteriously worked His way into my writing, even though I could not tell you where the family Bible was in the house. God had placed around me people who were quietly speaking His word into my life and it was finding its expression in my writing. My journal had found what was missing from my life, God.

So, all of this comes back around to my opening remark about finding the secret of successful writing. I know you are dying to know what it is. Successful writing is not about being published or making millions of dollars from your work. I will not lie, I would like to be able to make a living writing, but this is not why I write. In my journaling I had discovered that success was not something to pursue but was what is produced by a life which is surrendered to God. God has blessed me with many talents and abilities and my success in life comes from being a good steward of His gifts. What God has given to me is not meant to be hoarded for my own pleasure. God has blessed me so that I can live in a community of people and bless others. We all should benefit from each other's gifts and be a blessing using our talents and abilities to the fullest.

One way I am able to share what God has given is through my work in men's ministry. I have been actively involved in men's ministry for over 12 years. I use my talent and abilities in putting together Bible studies, Bible lessons, devotionals and short stories all for the honor of God and to share with people. I continue to grow and look to new ways of being a good steward of what God has given. Joining a writing group is one way I saw that I could improve in writing. I have learned a great deal from this very talented group of writers in Calhoun. Yet, I have gained so much more than just honing my writing skills. The friendships which have developed have done so much more for me. These relationships have enriched and shaped my life and given me encouragement, inspiration and motivation to do more with my writing than I would have on my own. The members of the Calhoun Writers Group have been a blessing to me and I pray I have blessed them as well. So, whether or not I ever get published or make one dime off anything I have written, my writing is successful in how it brings honor to God and has opened up pathways to some great relationships.

God Bless,
Gene

Elizabeth Amonett
CAW Founding Member

Dear Reader,
    I've always been a talker. As a young girl, I was shy, but once I got to know you, I could talk your ear off, or so I've been told.
    To this day, I can still fill up space around me with a constant stream of words. I can talk about any subject, too. And I really don't even have to know anything about it. I'm totally convinced that with the right words, spoken in love, words can heal the world. And if I cannot persuade you with my words, then more than likely, I'll confuse you or tire you out with my incessant talk until you finally surrender and let me have my way. Yes, I can talk, talk, talk!
    But writing? Well, looking back, since childhood, I've written. And yet, until recently, I've never considered myself a writer.
    (Please see the "Advice For Aspiring Writers" section of this anthology for a chattier version of my writing evolution called, "Dream a Little Dream". It began as my introduction letter, but it's been pushed to the back of the book because a writer friend said it was too long for a short introduction. My 'talking' case in point).
    So, for the purpose of this shorter introductory letter, let me *say*, my name is Elizabeth Amonett and I am a communicator.
    I have endless amounts of opinions, thoughts and story ideas tumbling around in my ever-aging, crowded mind. In an attempt to unclutter my brain from a tsunami of words, I've decided to try and organize these topics by filing them and then writing my beliefs down.

So... instead of talking at uninterested listeners or... to a wall, which I do not, by the way, literally talk to a wall, but I will, however, in the interest of full disclosure, confess that I do talk out loud in the car once in awhile when I'm the only person in it. Anyway... I digress. As I was *saying*, instead of talking out loud...Okay, who are we kidding, in addition to talking out loud..., I'm actively learning to better communicate my convictions in a comprehensible written format. Please read my entries in this book and decide for yourself if I've accomplished my goal.

Now... here's a scoop for you to consider. As confessed, I'm a talker, but please know, I'm also an avid reader and a good listener. So along with my own life experiences, I've gathered a mountain of information from reading and listening to others, and I have a whole lot to *say* and a whole lot to share. As my writing career moves forward, I hope you will stay with me, and maybe you can say, *"I knew her when"*.

From this point forward, my friend, I will try and speak less and hopefully write more. Who am I? Someone who wants to communicate and I'm looking for someone who wants to listen.

Sincerely,
Elizabeth Amonett

Vickie McEntire
CAW Founding Member

Dear Reader,

I am a daydreamer, a reader, and then, a writer. I believe to write; you must first be inspired. Inspiration doesn't come to you and beg to be told. It usually sneaks up on you while you are living life, like a cool breeze on a hot August day in the middle of a dry spell. As you pause to enjoy that moment, something happens inside of you that allows the mind to open. Good writing, the kind you can't put down, is led by the imagination. Yes, rules are important. Learn them and apply them, or break them, but tell the story with wild abandon.

Books were always within my reach. I remember gazing at a bookshelf the length of our hallway filled with three different sets of encyclopedias, the Childcraft set at my eye level. I am a book smeller from way back. It's a ritual I have maintained to this day— eyes closed, I take a quick inhale of the freshly printed pages. The words, almost as beautiful as the pictures, absorbed me and changed me. I read everything in the house, including the entire Bible cover to cover. My best friend lived across the road, and her mother was a reader. This woman had books stacked knee-high all over their house. I thought she was the luckiest woman in the world. I must have expressed such, because she soon started passing along books she no longer wanted. I inhaled them all.

Writing was just a natural extension of reading for me.

My dad was a minister. He wrote his sermons out, and unlike the other Baptist preachers of my childhood, his words were like poetry, soothing and flowing. He also wrote poems and stories for us kids on special occasions. My parents noticed my own desire to write and gave me an electric Brother typewriter for Christmas when I was in middle school. I stayed up late many a night click-clacking on that blue, plastic miracle machine.

Throughout my life, writing has been a natural complement to whatever I was doing from leaving notes for my children, to teaching Sunday School, to publishing a company newsletter. The older I get, the more I know that I was meant to tell stories through writing. I have been fortunate to have been published in Lady Literary Magazine and Calhoun Magazine. More of my stories can be found at ALiterateLife.blogspot.com, and my first children's book, *Baby Birds,* is available on amazon.com.

A major boost to my writing journey came after I joined Calhoun Area Writers. The encouragement and support of this group, and the critique group, have catapulted my words onto a larger platform. We have all learned so much from each other.

I would love to hear from you about your own journey, or what you think about our anthology. Send me an email at vickie.mcentire@comcast.net, or connect with me on Facebook.

Best wishes,
Vickie McEntire

Marla Aycock
CAW Member since 2015

Hello,

My name is Marla Aycock and I've been writing for an entire year. Aren't you impressed? (I started to put an exclamation point after the first sentence but I'm learning to use those *sparingly*, and mostly in dialogue—*Hrumph!*) So, we're talkin' gen-u-ine, *first time* author here.

I *am* a writer and future author—just a late bloomer, who some would label as a senior citizen of society, hot off the presses. As I enter my seventh decade, no one could be more surprised at the last statement than myself. Unlike many authors who knew from an early age they were *supposed* to write, I had *no* such inclination. Words scared me. Yes, you heard right. Words were scary to me. What if I said the wrong thing? What if I looked stupid? What if I hurt someone's feelings and destroyed their life? Words are powerful—like a sword. They can wound, defend, make you smile, belly-laugh, or cry.

Some people can carry on a conversation with a telephone pole. As a child, I watched in awe the motor-mouthed people in my life. Words flowed like an unending supply of water over Niagara Falls. Where were all the words coming from? How did they know what to say and when? Had they rehearsed? Since *my* thoughts were often labored in thick sludge before forming into words, I always felt a strong affinity to A. A. Milne's character, Winnie-the-Pooh, who was a *bit naïve and slow of thought.* So *quietly* I watched, listened, and learned.

An important critical move I've taken on my writing journey is to join the Calhoun Area Writers (C.A.W.) group a year ago. I immediately saw the value of their critique groups and adjusted my schedule to join one. This group continually prove to be invaluable to my writing process. The group itself is just "special!" Their warm and welcoming atmosphere drew me in, resulting in support and many new friends with similar ambitions.

From childhood, *most* authors are avid readers. Reading put *me* to sleep. I still use *light* reading to put myself to sleep, but now my night stand is surrounded by stacks of books I long to devour. Along my life's journey so many traumatic crazy events happened to me, I *had* to journal to survive. Recently the tragic loss of my youngest daughter pushed me from the silence of seven decades into loud and clamorous words. As I've written a raw and personal memoir of my daughter's life, I've found putting my emotional thoughts on paper was healing and even became exciting. Authors and knowledgeable literary friends said my writing was good and encouraged me. I found writing words on a page very different than *speaking* them. I could proofread, erase, rewrite, vent, or wad it up and throw it away. Now with technology, I can just hit *print* or *delete.*

The advantage about *this* late-blooming author is the rich layers of wisdom, seasons of life, and untold stories to draw from. A bit like an autumn flower; the surprising late bloomers have roots that have made it through the frigid winter, spring thaws, and simmering summers of life. They not only have a unique beauty with names like Aster, Sunflower, or Chrysanthemum—they are survivors, like Ironweed, Goldenrod, or—Marla

Whether you're needing some inspiration to spur you on through this crazy world we live in, or you need major encouragement to continue taking just one more baby step in the deepest trial of your life, I hope you'll be looking for the release of Esther's memoir, titled, "Supernaturally Natural." One of the most beautifully tragic stories you've ever read.
The Inspirational story, "Paradox of Joy" from my book is included in this Anthology. I hope you'll take a moment and check it out.
You can follow my progress on my FB page
or sign up for my Blog - https://goodgriefgal.wordpress.com/

I look forward to meeting you.

Marla Aycock

D.B. Martin
CAW Member since 2015

Dear Readers,

My name is David Brown / DB Martin. I am a designer and illustrator by trade. I came to Calhoun in 1984 from the United States Navy. I met and married a beautiful local girl and set up home. I love it here in Calhoun. I became a member of the Calhoun Area writers in early 2015. I was so pleased to find such a wonderfully talented group of writers in this area.

I have been writing for years and have been published under a number of personae, I was even on the staff of my high school paper. I have been published in many magazines: *Reader's Digest, Boys Life, Lady Bug, Highlights for Children,* and many others. I am excited about my first reporting article coming out in this October's issue of *Calhoun Magazine*.

I have written children's stories for most of my life but I began writing poetry a few years ago. I published my first collective book called HORRIBLE SANITY which I was amazed to see make the bestsellers list on Amazon for a short period.

One of my ultimate ambitions though, was to write a novel and in September of 2014, I published my first. Simply titled FEEDER, this was my first Horror novel and was happy to see it well received. I have just published the follow up book- actually a prequel to this story entitled MOTHER. These last two books I do not think I could have finished without the love, guidance and support of the members of this great group.

Please be aware when reading my stories, they tend to lean toward the macabre and deal with life, death and heaven and hell; subjects that are often controversial. These are tame in comparison to my norm, but I hope they make you think. Some that read may blush, others may point a judgmental finger in my direction but a few, if I have written it well, a choice few may even scream.

I hope you enjoy the stories within this collection and I hope you will check out my books which are available at your local bookstore, or Amazon. www.authordavidmbrown.com Thank you for reading.

Millicent Flake
CAW Member since 2015

I have had a writer inside of me all of my life, but she was afraid to come out. From the time I was a little girl, I had stories in my head and often lived more in a "make believe" world than in the real one. I'm sure much of this comes from the love of reading that was instilled in me by my parents and extended family. Books and reading have always been a huge part of my life.

However, like many of us, my creative outlets seemed to dry up as I reached my teenage years, and although I continued to love to read, writing seemed a frivolous hobby. I always kept a journal for my own personal emotional outlet, but it was a very private part of my life. As I entered adulthood and was absorbed with marriage, motherhood and working as a school media specialist, the writer inside me got pushed further down.

But she kept trying to get out. A few years ago, I got to know Ginger Anderson through a Bible Study at my church. She writes a hilarious and thought-provoking blog called *Ginger's Grocery*, and I confessed to her that I had always wanted to write. "Do it!" she exclaimed, and suddenly I had the courage to start.

I began writing a blog of devotional thoughts called *Under the Magnolia Tree*, named for my habit of sitting under the magnolia tree in my yard to read, and it has garnered a small following. I joined the Calhoun Area Writers and found more encouragement and inspiration. I've come to realize the importance of sharing my creative expression, and while I'm not sure where this writing journey is going, the author inside me is much happier.

My hope is that through this anthology you will find the courage to let loose whatever creative part of you is itching to get out, whether through music, art, photography or writing.

You can find Millicent's blog at maflake.wordpress.com.

Alana Kipe
CAW Member since 2016

Dear Future Author,

Life has been so very unexpected, as life usually is. By this point, it should really be expected to be so unexpected but yet we proceed to make big plans as though we are the author of life's agenda. As little as I prepared, I am a proud new mommy, illustrating books, taking on school, working full time and I guess now, I am an author as well! I won't mention my age, I am a lady after all, but I will say I am quite a youngin' too. Things can get pretty busy but throughout my hectic life, I am always saving a space for doing the things I love. Writing and painting are so very important to me and help me keep my sanity in this world. I guess what I am trying to say is, do *not* let *anything* hold you back from doing what you love. Be persistent, and never stop writing. I promise that even if you don't become a millionaire, you'll have a very rich life.

If you'd like to follow my work as an author or illustrator, you can email me at katkipe@gmail.com.

Enjoy, Alana Kipe

Mike Ragland
CAW Member since 2016

Mike Ragland was born and raised in Lindale, GA where he attended and graduated from Pepperell Schools.

After graduating from Pepperell High in 1963, he joined the Navy and was assigned to the submarine, *The USS Chopper* (SS-342) and served from '63 to '67. During that time, he served in the north Atlantic, Mediterranean, South America and throughout the east coast and Gulf of Mexico.

When Mike rejoined civilian life, he worked briefly laying carpet and was fired the day he planned to resign to join the Rome Police Department, where he served 40 years and retired as a Major. As a member of the force, he served as a motorcycle officer, patrol Sergeant, Shift Commander, and Captain in Charge of Detective Bureau. He also served as Juvenile Officer, as a liaison officer to Juvenile Court and Training Officer until 1999 when he was promoted to Major. As Major, he rotated serving the three major bureaus of the Police Department: Operations, Administration and Support Services. During that time he was also the principal grant writer for the Police Department, bringing in many Federal and State grants to secure police officer jobs, positions, and equipment, including the "*Call to Duty Monument*" that stands in front of the Rome Police Department today. He now serves as Councilman for the City of Cave Spring.

Mike was married to Martha Highfield on August 23, 1968, and they have one daughter, Bekki Ragland Fox, and two grandchildren, Caleb and Mattie Parris. He is an avid Crimson Tide and NASCAR fan. A much-loved speaker and writer in Northwest Georgia. Mike is devoted to writing full times since his retirement from the Police Department in April of 2007. He and his wife currently live in Cave Spring, GA along with three aggravating cats and three dachshunds.

His previous books are: *"Bertha"*, *"Legend of the Courage Wolf"*, and *"A Time to Gather Stones"* and current book, *"Living with Lucy"*.

Mike can be reached at mikeragland6@gmail.com.

Brian Grogan
CAW Member since 2016

I was born on Sunday June 12, 1960 at 3 am in Marietta Ga in Kennesaw hospital. I now live in Calhoun, GA. My early life was full of challenges and obstacles and at one point; my parents were told that I would never be able to take care of myself. Frustrated by dyslexia and other learning disabilities I had to learn and figure out how to think my way through life.

From this beginning, I began to perform a series of routines that I accomplish each morning and evening that helped me to turn my life around. I wrote a book, which is all about the power of living your life through the Daily Applications of Spiritual Principles. Spiritual principles are all about giving and the proper motive is not to be self-centered and cannot and should not be self-gratifying. When seeking to give to others I am thinking about what I have to give.
From sharing my thoughts each day on Facebook, I have found myself with roughly 3400 followers and 5000 friends, from all over the world in diverse countries reading the posts I create and commenting on them. My book is a compilation of those posts, separated by chapter into 10 Principles that have helped me to lead a better life and help others.

Brian's book, Daily Applications of Spiritual Principles, is published worldwide on Amazon and the US link is on Amazon at https://www.amazon.com/Daily-Applications-Unconditional-Love-Effectively/dp/1523206756

Karen Schmidt
CAW Member since 2016

Dear Reader,

I am a retired Registered Nurse, having worked in many different areas of nursing. I've been married for forty-eight years and have one adult daughter, two adult step-children, and two step-grandchildren. I am presently living in Georgia. Thank you for reading the anthology that includes my poem, UNKNOWN. I wrote it during one of the many times I was experiencing anxiety, pain, and insecurity about the future and have shared it many times with friends who have needed encouragement. I have learned that peace comes from leaving the outcome with God. I hope you find inspiration and peace from these words that come from my heart to yours.

Karen Schmidt

HERE IN GORDON COUNTY

Gordon County, home of the Calhoun Area Writers, is the last respite from the city sprawl of Atlanta to the south and Chattanooga to the north, with trucks barreling past on Interstate 75 and Florida-bound sunseekers stopping off for a fill-up. Rich with history, the Cherokee town of New Echota and the Civil War battlefield at Resaca are both state historic sites. Calhoun has grown in the last thirty years, but the downtown area retains its small town feel with a restored theater, active arts center, renovated library, and new shops and restaurants.

In this section, we are sharing some of our experiences living in this beautiful part of Georgia, where the Appalachian Mountains begin as hills and the Conasauga, Coosawattee, and Oostanaula rivers meander. What would you like to share about your hometown?

Spirits of the Harbour House
By Millicent Flake

"Do you have ghosts in your house?" The woman asked the question in all earnestness.

I hesitated with my answer. I was telling her about my antebellum home, which has stood proudly in Northwest Georgia for over a hundred and fifty years. Do we have the sounds of chains and moaning in the attic, doors that unexpectedly slam shut, whispers in the night? No, not those sorts of ghosts.

But I feel the spirits of the house every day.

Known in Sugar Valley as the old Harbour House, our house began its life in 1859 when the area was still wilderness, only recently inhabited by the Cherokee who farmed and hunted along Snake Creek. Situated on a slight rise with Horn Mountain at its back, the simple farmhouse was built to face the morning sun to the east. Slaves may have helped to fell the huge trees that became the walls and floors, and to haul the native stone that was used for the foundation. Originally designed as a "dog-trot" with two rooms on each side of a central hallway, the breeze would have blown through from front to back and cooled off hot summer days.

According to Jewell Reeves' history of Gordon County, *Climb the Hills of Gordon,* the house was begun by G. Winn, one of the first settlers in the Valley. He was a trustee for the Gordon

County Male and Female Seminary, located in Sugar Valley, which offered young men the opportunity to learn subjects such as letter writing, Latin, astronomy, philosophy and civil engineering. Girls were instructed by Mrs. Skelly, the principal's wife, in reading, writing, arithmetic and French, as well as the skills of sewing and embroidery. Many of the prominent men of the community were on the board of trustees, including Hammy Harbour and James Wright. What would later become Sugar Valley Baptist Church had already been established for over twenty years by 1859, with these same men as its leaders. As they formed a new community, these founding families valued church and education and worked hard to provide both for their children.

Following the Civil War, James and Louisa Wright bought the house and lived there for about twenty years, raising their eight children. According to Mrs. Reeves, they moved to Rome in 1887 for their daughters to attend Shorter College, even though most girls did not even go to grammar school at the time. Their daughter Gorda married Will Harbour, son of Hammy, and moved into the house, where they farmed and raised their children Hudson and Psyche. Hudson grew up and married Maude Quillian in the early 1900's and they inherited the house and the acres of farmland surrounding it. With their only child Elroy, Maude and Hudson lived out their lives in the house as farmers and community leaders. Hudson owned most of the farmland in the Valley and was the superintendent of Sugar Valley Baptist Church. Maude attended the Methodist Church and had a store a mile away in the downtown area. The house was a showplace in the community, full of beautiful antiques.

Louisa, Gorda and Maude each fashioned the house and furnishings to the era in which she lived. Louisa added French doors to the front and Gorda extended the front porch and added a large dining room with picture windows and a small kitchen and pantry. Maude changed the porches back to their original size and added a bathroom and covered sunporch. Each family upgraded and modernized, from electricity and telephones to indoor plumbing and gas heat.

Through the years, the sounds of phonographs, radio, and television broke the quiet of the countryside. Horses and buggies were replaced with rumbling cars and airplanes and their sounds mingled with the whistle of the train as it brought goods and passengers from Calhoun, Rome and Dalton to Sugar Valley.

My husband and I were house hunting in 1988 and from the moment I saw the Harbour House I knew I was meant to be here. Almost thirty years later I feel a connection to Louisa, Gorda and Maude like a satin ribbon running through the years, binding us through our love for our home.

They have left behind reminders of their time, such as the small lace up shoes we found in the attic that a young girl might have worn in the 1890's. Did these belong to Psyche Harbour, and were put aside as she outgrew them? In the concrete of the front steps is inscribed *Elroy Harbour 192_*, with the last number broken off. I picture Elroy as a child in his short pants, the cement wet from the workers' trowel, placing his mark with a stick or a screwdriver as the new porch is being finished. And in the root cellar under the side porch we found jars still holding the tomatoes and green beans that someone had canned many summers before.

Perhaps my greatest link to these homemakers is the collection of broken pottery and dishes we found as we tilled our garden behind the house. From thick green ash-fired pieces dating to the 1800's to shards of delicate china, these remnants spark my imagination of day-to-day life years ago. How did they end up buried under several inches of rich soil and what caused them to break in the first place? Did an argument between husband and wife result in a thrown plate? Did a toddler, in the days before plastic sippy-cups, drop his bowl to the floor to see it bounce? Or like many of my dishes over the years, did the mug slip through soapy hands and break in the dishpan?

Louisa. Gorda. Maude. On quiet summer mornings when I hear the birds chirping, a distant rooster crowing, and the bees buzzing in the ancient magnolia tree, I think of them and wonder if they listened to these same sounds. Did they watch the sun set over the mountain after a hard day's work, perhaps lifting their long skirts so that they could catch a breeze? Did they hear the laughter of their children as they played in the cool water of the nearby creek or watch them catch lightning bugs in the summer evenings? Did they feel the same sense of pride and happiness that I do each time they rounded the curve in the road and saw the house waiting for them?

Someday it will be our turn to pass the house along to the next family, who will have their share of happiness and grief, laughter and tears. Just as in years past, I hope the house will again hear the sounds of babies laughing and children running through its rooms. As the new woman of the Harbour House takes hold of the satin ribbon connecting those of us who have loved it for over 150 years, I hope she will listen to the bees high in the magnolia tree on summer mornings and watch as the sun sets behind Horn Mountain, bringing another day to an end. My spirit will be mingling with those who have gone before and speaking to her.

Sources: Reeve, J. B. (1997). Climb the Hills of Gordon (2nd ed., Vol. I). Greenville, SC: Southern Historical Press.

My Calhoun
By Vickie McEntire

When you ask a Southerner to tell a story about the past, the timeline is sure to be sprinkled with phrases like before my time, back in the day, when I was knee-high to a grasshopper, many moons ago, or now-a-days. These markers allow the recollection to flow without interruption for lack of a specific date. With that said, where my research, and memory, have failed to provide a specific date, enjoy the Southern mile markers on this look back at my hometown.

I took my first breath after a quick slap to my behind by Dr. Robert D. Walter. That was how they welcomed babies into the world back in the day. That was in September of 1965. Back then, Gordon County Hospital was located on Pine Street. Dr. Walter and his wife, Margaret "Mac" Caroline McClain, had moved to Calhoun in 1937. He joined Drs. Hall and Johnston in serving the community at the Johnston-Hall Hospital on South Wall Street, which moved in 1953 to the facility where I was born. For years, we continued to see our doctors at their offices in the Johnston-Hall building. The old wood floors creaked under your feet, the wide halls were lined with dark, wooden benches, and a strong smell of antiseptic welcomed you at the door.

Before my time, the young people hung out at the A&W Root Beer Drive-In on Highway 41 North, in the vicinity of where Tierce's Little Giant grocery store is located now. My mama, Frances (Stansell) Ray, fondly remembered working there when she was a teenager in the early '60s. The customers would pull into the gravel parking lot and flash their headlights to get service, which prompted a car hop to walk over and take their order. Steaming hot Papa Burgers®, Coney hot dogs with chili and cheese, and frosty cold root beer floats in thick glass mugs were delivered to the customer on a silver tray that hooked onto the top of their partially rolled-down window. All the while, the voice of Elvis crooned from the radio.

When I was knee-high to a grasshopper, my best friend, Melanie, lived across the road. We enjoyed wholesome fun like playing in the yard barefoot, climbing trees, and riding our bikes (without helmets) miles from home. We only checked in for meals, and took breaks under shade trees to catch our breath and guess what the clouds revealed to us. The first day school was out we kicked off our shoes, and they didn't go back on for the rest of the summer. There was no clock to watch, no digital devices to distract. We stayed outside until it was dark, then we tried to catch "lightening bugs" to put in glass jars topped with metal lids we had slashed holes in with a kitchen knife. We were free to be creative, so we played house, beauty shop, church. We put on plays for our families. We made up songs and dance routines to our favorite music.

On lucky days, our family of six children went swimming in the ice-cold creek water at The Pocket Recreation Area at the foot of John's Mountain. To keep them chilled, we put our drinks and watermelon in the spring-fed water. That water was so cold our lips would be turning blue by the time we were forced to get out of the creek. We rode home with the windows down, and the hot wind blowing into the car made us drowsy.

We counted down the days waiting for the Christmas lights to be turned on in downtown Calhoun. It was a tradition for many families on Thanksgiving night to drive to town to see the strings of big colored bulbs, which were strung from one side of the street across to the other. Daddy drove our station wagon slowly down Wall Street, while we stretched our necks trying to see all the different decorations and the majestic live tree in front of the Courthouse.

Years later, I took my own children downtown to see the lights. Santa waited patiently at Super-D on Court Street, while I tried to convince my crying two-year-old to sit on his lap. We went to the back of the store to take a seat on a stool at the counter and order some delicious food. I can still smell the grilled cheese and deep-fried hot dogs. Rows and rows of shelves reached to the ceiling with everything from toys to food to artificial Christmas trees, silver tinsel and a three-foot tall nativity for your front yard.

My early education began at Belwood Elementary School, which is located across from Calhoun Premium Outlets. Many moons ago, the school was the only building on that road, and it was much smaller. The teachers wrote with chalk on chalkboards and turned a crank handle to open the huge windows in the spring. Every Friday was ice-cream day. My friend and I brought ten cents each to purchase a creamy chocolate Fudgesicle®. Back then, the ice cream had two sticks and was indented in the middle—perfect for sharing! We played Red Rover, Red Rover, Simon Says, and Red Light, Green Light during our daily time on the playground. Later, in a woodshop class at Ashworth Middle School, which is now Gordon Central, I made a checkerboard out of two different types of wood. I still have it. I guess it would be considered vintage now; to me it's priceless.

As I got older, I felt the urge to be independent. A big step in that direction was to earn my own money, so I started a Grit paper route on Tucker Hollow Road. I acquired my first real job the year I went into ninth grade at Calhoun High School. I walked to that job every day, rain or shine. I remember falling asleep in Coach Tucker's math class, which was right after lunch, because I was tired from working the night before at the Yellow Jacket. By the way, they still have the best cheeseburgers and strawberry milkshakes in town! I learned to type the phrase, *now is the time for all good men to come to the aid of their country*, at 80 words per minute in Mrs. McCarver's Vocational Office Training class.

My teenage years were filled with hay rides around Blackwood Church Cemetery, weenie roasts with the youth group of Boone Ford Baptist Church, cheerleading camp at the University of Georgia, slumber parties, going to the Northwest Georgia Regional Fair and school dances. Our senior play was The Sound of Music, which is still my all-time favorite musical. A favorite hangout was Pasquale's, which was located in the Gordon Hills Shopping Center. They had the best salads and cheese sticks and lasagna…gosh I miss that place!

I hope you have enjoyed this brief visit back to the Calhoun of my childhood. Regardless of where you are from—north, south, east, west, or across the ocean—I encourage you to write your own hometown story. I promise, there are folks who will be delighted to read it.

Calhoun's Magnificent Mystery Writer
By Amber Lanier Nagle

It's a gift. She weaves her mysteries with flair and panache, dropping-in enough detail to make them both believable and beloved. Mignon Franklin Bailard is a natural-born storyteller, which doesn't surprise anyone who knows even a little bit about her background. Born and raised in Calhoun, the mystery writer's younger years were steeped in creativity, camaraderie, and an unbridled freedom to explore the world around her.

"Our house was near the intersection of North Wall Street and East Line Street—where CVS Pharmacy sits today," Ballard remarks. "My sister [Sue Marie Franklin Lewis] and I were children during World War II. It was a simpler time, and our parents gave us free rein, just as long as we stayed out of trouble and checked in from time to time. We roamed the streets on our bikes and roller skates looking for the next great adventure."

Perhaps it was during this time that Ballard developed her voracious appetite for mystery and drama. She and her sister, along with a small band of neighborhood playmates, spent their Saturday afternoons watching Westerns at the GEM Theatre and their Sunday afternoons listening to their parents and aunts tell stories. During the other days of the week, the group of friends created their own entertainment.

"We were creepy children with large imaginations," she says. "We made peanut butter and crackers and walked up to Fain Cemetery. We sat outside the Pitts family mausoleum and told ghost stories. And sometimes, we pretended to have a funeral in the basement of a neighbor's house. They had a wind-up record player and one cracked record of The Indian Love Call that we used as the funeral music."

According to Ballard, they took turns playing the different characters of the funeral—the widow, the preacher, the mourners, and of course—the corpse. She and her friends would would pretend to stand at the graveside and whoever was playing the preacher's part would say, "Today we are gathered to say our final farewells to this man. He was a very good man."

"And then, whoever was pretending to be the deceased would start rising-up and grabbing at all of us," she laughs. "And we would all start screaming and running away. We were just crazy kids."

They also sat below the green neon sign of nearby Combs Funeral Home and told ghost stories in the eerie glow of the sign's light. But their escapades didn't always involve the macabre. The friends also hung from the branches of a friend's magnolia tree and played Tarzan. One of Ballard's friends had mastered yodeling the distinctive, ululating Tarzan call. And they reenacted scenes from Ali Baba and Forty Thieves. It was as childhood rich in imagination. Ballard's parents were Bernard and Mignon Harlan Franklin of Calhoun. Her father served in France during World War I, then returned home where he farmed, commanded the local National Guard, and eventually became the postmaster. Indeed, the National Guard Armory is named for Ballard's father. Her maternal grandparents owned the mercantile store where TJ's Office Supply stands today. Ballard's best friend, Tommye Lewis (she's Tommye Johnston now), lived just a block away from her house. The two were inseparable companions as children and still remain best friends.

"I went to grammar school where the First Baptist Church is now," she recalls. "I still remember looking out of the windows in first grade and watching some men put up the swings and the slide and the climb-around in the playground. I was so excited."
She started attending Calhoun High School in eighth grade, and after school dismissed, the young Ballard worked at the library where she was surrounded by books.

"The library used to be a log cabin," she recalls. "And there was a porch covered in a wisteria vine. I worked for Ms. Tarvin."

She also worked for *The Calhoun Times*, and Ballard still remembers a day at the newspaper when she was working up front with Roy McGinty.

"A man came in wearing shorts and a Hawaiian shirt and said, 'I'd like to put an ad in the paper—I want to place a reward for the man who ran off with my wife. When I find him, I'm going to kill him,'" Ballard recalls. "And then he lifted his shirt, and he had a gun. Mr. McGinty told me to get in the back, and I did, but I couldn't wait to get home and tell my parents all about it. That was a pretty exciting day for little Calhoun."

After graduating from Calhoun High School in 1952, Ballard earned a degree in journalism from the University of Georgia. She worked for a short time at the Atlanta Journal and Constitution (AJC).

"It was a time when writing opportunities for females were somewhat limited," she says. "I worked in the Women's Department and edited a few pieces penned by Celestine Sibley."

While working at the AJC, she also met the dashing Gene Ballard, who worked in the advertising department. The two married and moved to Decatur. They raised two daughters, Melissa and Amy.

"Being a writer is all I ever wanted to do," she says. "So after my youngest daughter went to kindergarten, I sat down and started writing. My first book was a children's book, and I never sold it. But I kept writing, and I eventually sold a few short stories to children's magazines."

The young family moved to Fort Mill, South Carolina, and Ballard kept her imagination and her pen in motion. She received her first book contract for Aunt Matilda's Ghost, a mystery for young readers. Eight years later, she sold Raven Rock, her first mystery for adults. After publishing five more stand-alone adult mysteries, she sold The War in Sallie's Station. Then in 1999, Ballard introduced the world to her beloved angel-sleuth, Augusta Goodnight. Six more heavenly mysteries featuring Augusta Goodnight followed in the series before Ballard moved on to her next project.

She penned a mystery series set during World War II based on the fictional character, Miss Dimple. Her stories swirl with colorful characters and warm Southern humor. And for local readers who feel that the fictitious town of Elderberry, Georgia sounds a little too familiar, it should.

"Sure, I drew upon my memories of Calhoun while I was writing," she says. "My main character [Miss Dimple Kilpatrick] is not based on any one particular person, but perhaps she is a combination of many teachers and people I knew growing up in Calhoun."

In August of 2016, Ballard's newest creation was released. Miss Dimple and the Slightly Bewildered Angel is a treat for both Augusta Goodnight fans and Miss Dimple followers, as Ballard's book has the two women teaming up to solve a murder mystery.

Aside from her mystery writing, Ballard also wrote the script and lyrics for Bandstand Tales, a musical about Fort Mill. She loves acting.

"I do enjoy being on the stage but have been mostly in the chorus or with very small speaking parts," she says. "A few years ago, I did have a larger speaking role in a one-act mystery in which I had to die on stage. All of my stage experience has been on the local level at community theaters."

Years ago, Ballard was an extra in a three-part television series, Chiefs, starring Charlton Heston which was filmed near Fort Mill.

Ballard moved back to Calhoun a few years ago, and we are so glad she did. She jumped right into community life and helps numerous causes around town.

"I wanted to be closer to my daughters and their families," she says. "And Calhoun will always be home to me. It will always be in my heart."

POETRY

Poetry. There's something uniquely human about it, isn't there? It touches us down deep in that soulish part of us that separates us from all other living things. Poetry has been part of the human experience since our earliest literary history. As soon as we, mankind, discovered that we could communicate through the written word, we began creating poetry in one form or another. From as far back as 1500 B.C., when the Aryans created their Sacrificial Hymns, we have expressed ourselves through verse.

Then Homer came along with the sweeping narratives of his great epic poems.

And Sophocles thrilled (and frightened) Athens with his tragedies.

King David reached for the sublime in his Psalms.

William Wordsworth. Emily Dickinson. Robert Frost. Alfred Lord Tennyson. Maya Angelo. Even Dr. Seuss. These, and so many others, have poured out their thoughts and dreams and feelings in poetry. Through their work, we see the world in fresh, new ways, and even, sometimes, understand ourselves better. Whether it's the cryptic haiku, the elegant sonnet, the lilting limerick or the unbounded flow of free verse, we can lose ourselves in the sheer beauty of the words.

Now, we're not claiming that we are poets in the same league as those mentioned above. Not at all. But we do think we have something to say, too. And we very much want to share that with you. So, pour a fresh cup of coffee, find a comfy chair, put your feet up and let our words wash over you.

Read on. And enjoy.

Sea of Poison Words
By Alana Kipe

She stands.
The damp grains of what used to be, press under her.
Unformed pieces of glass cover her toes.
She smiles
at the slow uprising of possibilities that wash in over her feet.
She stands
and
She watches
it return, taking with it all that is around her.
She thinks
of how interesting she will seem be as part of it.
She steps forward.
The water bends the tips of its fingers into its palm to draw her in.
She steps in further.
She feels an underlying tone of danger that she ignores
and
She continues.
The soft brushing sounds are now a crash that yells hateful things
around her.
She closes her ears.
Her heart beats fast and though she is afraid,
She does not stop.
The ground that was familiar was slips from under her.
She begins to become part of this formless body.
The crashes now hit her chest harder than before, pushing her
backward.
She falls
and
She sinks.
It pulls her in farther, slowly as her lungs fill with the unfamiliar
pain.
She is but a few feet under and if only she had known,
the straightening of her legs would prevent a fate so unkind.
She could return to the happy land she knows if she would just

Take A Stand.
Her thoughts almost final until she decides she has had enough.
She fights.
Swinging her arms and feet against the force
She doesn't give in
and then
She Stands.

Things to Never Do
By Paul Moses

I have learned the hard way of things to never do,
Like never make a ladle of a running shoe.

And don't taste cat litter just because it's there;
You might cough a fur ball that's not completely hair.

And never try to hang-glide from a chimney top;
You'll just think you're flying, til the concrete makes you stop.

Never, ever, ride a cow, although they look quite tame;
Bovines are not adverse, it seems, to making you quite lame.

Get your honey from a jar, not from a living hive,
And you might have your morning toast stingless and alive.

Please don't tell your grandma she has a big backside,
Unless you like the dickens beaten from your hide.

All these things, and others, I've learned are not the way
To get along with others and thrive another day.

Contentment Curse
By Paul Moses

I'm cursed with contentment;
I simply don't care
If my leaky roof drips
And waters my hair.

If my holly bush grows
As tall as a tree
And blots out the sunshine
That's all right with me.

I'm cursed with contentment;
I'm happy to let
The hedges reach higher
And reach higher yet.

If vines choke my roses,
My lawn goes to seed,
It all gives me more shade
In which I can read.

Genie
By Paul Moses

Magic Genie, make me happy!
Leave your lamp and make it snappy!
I have big demands for you
To make my fondest wish come true.

Magic Genie, I'm your master!
I demand that you move faster!
Come out now and show your power;
Make me rich this very hour!

Magic Genie, what's that you say?
You turn brats into frogs each day?
I want my wish! Give it! Give it!
What's the hold up? Ribbit! Ribbit!

Destiny Pondered
By Paul Moses

Destiny pondered the purpose of man;
Was it all random or part of a plan?
Were we but minions and pawns and such things,
Poor helpless victims, like puppets on strings?
Destiny wondered if death was a date
With the Almighty, or was it just Fate?
She quizzed a rabbi, a pastor, a priest,
A doctor of Plato and ten more at least.
She studied the Bible, some scrolls, the Quran,
Destiny weighed out this learn-ed advice;
Was it all God or rolls of the dice?
She pestered a turbaned imam from Iran,
Consulted the Aztecs (their Runes for a clue),
And old Chinese proverbs and Poor Richard's too.
She read Aristotle, Plutarch, and the stars,
Channeled the Buddha, Confucius and Mars.
reached a conclusion: "That's it! Oh what luck!"
"I've figured it out!" ...and was hit by a truck.

Eleanor's Lament
By D.B. Martin

Sit down now and calm yourselves,
For this will not last for long.
But it must be told and told tonight,
Before the midnight song.
Fear not for the tale before you,
Lies but in the past.
Its hunger has long been sated,
Its players have all been cast.
I will reveal the tale,
And I will recite it right and true.
And tell it as the lines have run,
Within the crimson hue.
Tell me more my Eleanor,
Tell me what you will.
And know that I love you so,
So much that I will kill.
In her hair were auburn curls,
That bounced along the shore.
Oh, what emerald eyes,
Were our Eleanor.

A pleasant smile an alluring gait,
She held along the boards.
Inspiring without intent,
As she wandered along the shores.
She stepped down from the boards,
And walked along the sands.
And tilt her head toward heaven,
As the wind blew her curls to strands.
She stood upon the border there,
Between the sand and the sea.
Gazing out with a longing,
And with a whisper set it free.
Her yearning seemed so simple,
A meager thing to ask.
For her wistful dreams were of love,

A love to always last.
What burning were the fire's,
How upon her soul they pour.
Oh, what love's desires,
Were our Eleanor.

The words had scarcely passed her lips,
When turning she did find.
A boy with lovely sable eyes,
Standing just behind.
His smile fell upon her,
Along with his gaze.
And her heart it went a flutter,
Within the summer's haze.
Their love it bloomed as a lily,
Seemingly overnight.
A playful love, a magical love,
Like cast from a sprite.
They joined their love beneath the moon,
Where they met upon the sand.
Their eyes never parting,
In loving holding hands.
Now she was consumed by love,
Embracing to the core.
Oh, what loving smiles,
Were our Eleanor.

Then one day within their home,
She had dressed herself with care.
To make it smart and beautiful,
For the loving pair.
She found it dog eared and tattered,
Hidden within his bureau drawer.
A letter from her to him,
The one she so adored.
It spoke of times they had,
And moments that they shared.
Moments they had stolen from her,
And the fury in her flared.
This was the one she'd gave her heart,

And even gave her soul.
And now to find it was lie,
Left her heart and empty hole.
So she dropped down to the boards,
And cried and she deplore.
Oh, What Horrid Truths,
Were our Eleanor.

Simply blind to her heart's mistake,
She saw him only with love's new eyes.
Never cautious, never doubting,
That his words were purled with lies.
Now with the truth exposed,
Broadly her at her feet.
She felt her heart was dying,
Slowing down with every beat.
How could he she cried,
Take their love and wrought.
For him to do what he has done,
Their love to him means naught.
Now lost within the tear stained words,
That laid within her palm.
The anger built within her soul,
And became a burning calm.
How the pain it thrived,
From the one she dared adore.
Oh, what heart that breaks,
Were our Eleanor.

Her rage had grown in torrents,
When he opened their chamber door.
Who is she, she screamed at once,
As she rose up from the floor.
He saw within her hand,
The words he had kept.
And knew that he had sinned,
And the conclusion would accept.
She threw her arms against his chest,
And screamed I loved you, why.
I hate you for what you've done she said,

And I wish that you would die.
He backed away in horror,
At the harshness of her phrase.
Then fell through the window pane,
In a momentary daze.
She watched in terror as he fell below,
And two stories hit the floor.
Oh, what sorrow's tears,
Were our Eleanor.

She ran down to his side,
Crying hard and crying strong.
Begging for forgiveness,
From the man who did her wrong.
She knelt down by his side,
And the tears how they ran.
And all she felt was pity,
For this beast of a man.
I prayed for our love she said,
And I will never leave you, never.
For the promise of our love,
Is that it will always last forever.
She held him gently by his face,
And looked into his eyes.
And gently kissed the man she loved,
As he drifts away and dies.
Now alone within this world,
She cursed at God and swore.
Oh, what anger brings,
Were our Eleanor.

There are no stars that dab the skies,
Within the boundaries of the urban lights.
There wrapped within the glimmer bloom,
The skies refuse the nights.
But there lie far beneath the city streets,
Shadows without souls.
Where death beats their empty hearts,
And sorrow fills their holes.
They live within the darkness,

In a life without love.
Damned by mistakes in life,
Cursed by him above.
And there from this darkness,
To walk again once more.
Rising from the bowels of hell,
He came for Eleanor.
How unknowing how unfair,
Of what love held in store.
Oh, what love's rewards,
Were our Eleanor.

She stood where they met upon the sand,
Gazing out across the sea.
And turned and stared in horror,
Of what just could not be.
There slowly moving within the dark,
It slid across the sand.
Calling out her name,
And reaching out its hand.
Eleanor I love you,
I need you it did shrill.
I need you Eleanor,
I need to make you still.
Tell me more my Eleanor,
Tell me what you will.
And know that I love you so,
So much that I would kill.
No she screamed it cannot be,
The one that I adore.
Oh, what horrors,
Were our Eleanor.

She ran along the darkened beach,
To a skid upon the sand.
Crying as she climbed aboard,
And pushed it from the land.
From the skid where she sailed,
She could hear it's howling still.
It's begging and it's pleading,

And it's mournful crying shrill.
She still could see,
Its fingers ever outward reaching.
And hear his mournful cries,
Of his forever screeching.
Screaming as it slid slowly within sea,
Calling out forevermore.
Reaching out, crying out,
I love you, Eleanor.
She screamed into the night,
At the death covered gore.
Oh, what mournful cries,
Were our Eleanor.
Then only in a moment,
He was lost beneath the tide.
And the night it became silent,
As she settled down and cried.
Then there from within the depths,
He rose from in under.
Screaming out her name again,
As he pulled the boat asunder.
Eleanor my love,
He screamed into the night.
As he stared from within the water,
With a smile dressed in smite.
She turned away and screamed,
As she swam swiftly toward the shore.
Crying out within the night,
Frightened to the core.
She swam with everything she had,
Screaming all the more.
Oh, what hells,
Were our Eleanor.

She could still hear him calling,
Screaming out her name.
Eleanor my lovely bride,
It is you I've come to claim.
Then there beneath the briny waters,
He rose within her face.

As she screamed in mortal terror,
As his clutch now stopped the chase.
Then covered deep in gore,
He kissed his frozen bride.
And pulled them both beneath the waves,
Where our Eleanor, she died.
Your dreams have now come true,
Love forevermore.
Oh, what promise's kept,
Were our Eleanor.

Chimera
By D.B. Martin

Stagnate hollow cries, flourish solid from the wood.
And I began to understand, that they were all misunderstood.
My desire to assist, only ignites my solemn cumber,
But pushes me much closer, as it pulls me from my slumber.
As I stand within my own, unable to support,
And gain the strength needed, before my bravery was thwart.
The cries called out again, sheer silent in the night,
And through the blinding glow, a vision I caught sight.
There within this vision, darkness did unfold,
A searing sight to see, but the blossom it was cold.
Once again I staid, excited in my thought,
Fearful of the night, that myself I could not wrought.
The rule it was gone, it unfolded as it will,
Do I run for my life, or am I standing there still.
Then the reflection it was gone, and the disdain became clear,
As the cries came again, causing thoughts to cohere.
And as these thoughts dispersed, my mind slowly did amass,
As the fear ran up behind, and I moved to let it pass.
What anguish was being contrived, and what delight did it bring,
And what hell was in the silence, between the songs that they sing.
The vision it still blazed, foreign from my home,
As I stared through the glass, neglectful to roam.
Then darkness from within, outside it dilate,
Till my heart nearly stopped, and my breath abbreviate.
The shadow it raises high, dwarfing my lair,
As I closed my eyes and pray, that it really wasn't there.
Upon my humble dwelling, revealing slowly did swathe,
As I turned in uncertain circles, like wood upon the lathe.
I grabbed my hair and pulled, as I pushed the fear within,
Then I heard there in the silence, the crying once again.
Sounds without pleasure, a mournful kind of whine,
The I saw within the glass, that the screaming it was mine.

Then the shadow it grew silent, within the cadence of my call,
As I pulled the sheets around me, wrapped within my funeral pall.
And I watched the shadows now bright within the night,

Taunting and teasing and moving with delight.
I saw unfounded as it was, truly it was there,
The shadow was within, as it broke the window's glare.
I floundered and I falter, reversing from the glass,
And faced away from my affliction, praying it would pass.
Then warm like the fingers of a ghost, within a winter's mist,
Its core I could feel, as upon my skin the cold it kissed.
My hand loosely screened my eyes, as my face it went taut,
And my movements to be freed, were found to be naught.
I screamed I trust no more, as my anxiety did amass,
And was poised to recoil, but a wall I met alas.
With my rampart now invaded, a depression did appear,
And calmness overtook me, as I bathed within the fear.
I leered within the room, disbelief draped in candlelight,
As the shadow did move closer, merely brightening my plight.

Closer and closer, from the light grew the grey,
And daunted as I was, I let forth a maddening bray.
Why torment me I pleaded, what pleasure does this bring,
Does it lessen your pain, why upon me this hell do you fling.
And I fell there weeping, beneath this vision ascending in the air,
And searched within the flaw, for some principle to wear.
A reason or a cause, for my ineptness to comprehend,
Some anticipation for escape, from the one who lays penned.
But from the shadow and air, there came not a word,
But somewhere in the silence, the answer was heard.
As the shadow moved to the right, the left was undisturbed,
But my fear it held me captive, so my fleeing it was curbed.
Then somewhere in the darkness, my strength it gained sight,
And I leapt from the floor, and I ran out into the night.
Hands reaching out in front not looking toward the after,
Screaming through the silence, amidst my own demented laughter.
Blindly through blackness, the uncertainty revealed,
As the limbs tore at my flesh, and my skin it was peeled.
But I ran and ran, for in fear I could not cease,
My heart pounded steady, and my face turned cerise.
And even though I avoided, even a meager glance,
A simple turn of the head, the slightest askance.
I knew without fail, what was ascending upon,
And I dared not look back, to see what nightmare was drawn.

Then the breath of the forest, turned from still to gale,
And the trees pitched, as I moved through the vale.
I could feel it abaft, every step forward without care,
And it knew without question that I was completely aware.
And the blood ran from my face, as my tongue stopped to taste,
The first casualty it thought, and this blessing I embraced.
Knowing there I was, here within this hellish night,
Was astonishing in itself, and I clutched at the smite.
Then it passed and stood before me, and I ceased within my tracks,
And I stood there quite stolid, looking back upon my cracks.
There standing tall above it, perched within the light of morrow,
Stood a cupola and delicate steeple rising from a house of sorrow.
There was no contentment in the shadow, it was heated you could
see,
But the understanding of just what it wanted, was a mystery to me.
Sanctuary mere steps away, yet it stood within my path,
Then a calmness overtook me, for I did not wish to test its wrath.
Tell me Oh spirit, what is the substance of your desire,
Why disperse around me, from me what will you acquire.
Then in the disorder of the twilight, the design became clear,
And within the clarity of the image, within me grew a blinding fear.
For moving from the darkness, came the image of dread,
Run if you will, for I have come for the dead.

Willow Woods
By D.B. Martin

There lies a place, near to here,
where darkness dwells and does not veer.
Where who so wanders beneath the veil,
lies forever within the pale.
Where lovers often wander in,
to hide beneath,
to forge a sin.
Traverse and amble, thinking not,
whilst body and soul, ever rot.
And though they beckon, through constant screams,
to haunt our thoughts and invade our dreams.
Like the rain of God,
they drop from the heavens,
to play in sixes, never sevens.
And those that venture, in its midst,
never loved, never kissed.
Dared to walk within the vein,
Find not fortune, only bane.
For beneath the moss, mud and insect bite,
lie the demons, that forever fright.
For within Willow Woods,
where branches bend,
and from the heavens,
do descend.
To drag and dangle,
grasp and seize,
reaching, pulling,
to appease.
That which dwells, within the wood,
and adorns itself,
bough as hood.
Pulling souls with good intent,
to bend as do,
branches bent.
Pulling down,
to asunder,
where there is no light,

merely thunder.
Beneath the soil,
beneath the root,
where stone and earth,
both dilute.
And Hell is formed,
from Willow's feet,
and souls are thrashed,
as devil's wheat.

What I Found in Santa's Beard
By Marla Aycock

Santa's Beard is so revealing, white and soft and so appealing.
But under a microscope we'd find, a single strand would blow your mind.
Is it natural, is it bleached? Maybe he should be impeached.

Is he ancient, just how old? His beard this mystery unfolds.
Examining his telomeres, we'll find exactly what appears.
Like plastic tips on shoelaces, they hold mystery unknown for ages.
The science of chromosomes and DNA,
might reveal the magic of his long-term stay.

Where was Santa's actual birth? Was it here on planet earth?
Lapland, Europe or the USA?
We find science has a say.
Analyzing, comparing, peoples far and wide
Scientific evidence will provide.
And with a little luck and biology, we may find his family genealogy.

Does he really drink the spirits left out for him?
That single strand of beard, even reveals this whim?
We look for tannins and find this preference too.
I can see him now shouting out, "WooHoo!"

Does he live at the North Pole all year long?
Again, to the lab...can't get this wrong!
Hair is like a sponge you see,
soaking up pollutants from A to Z.

Checking out hair from different parts of the world
matching the toxins whether straight or curled,
We'd know Santa's location each month of the year.
We'd discover his movements whether there or here.

But air in the Lapland is squeaky clean
so this strand would be, politically "green".
His beard would be pure except one spike,

which would be the moments of Christmas night.

Last but not least does his beard reveal
what he actually eats at most every meal?
Amazing what science and a microscope make known,
Trace metals are found where food is grown.
Matching them to Santa's beard
you have to laugh, it's just plain weird.
Whether Santa is carnivore or vegetarian,
I doubt he eats much venison.

What I Found in Santa's Beard
By Karli Land

I was looking for cookies,
At least a small crumb
Maybe some sugar plums
Or a big ball of gum

I thought I'd find pie
Maybe apple or cherry
I looked for turkey and gravy
I searched for a hint of cranberry

I was sure there would be snowflakes
And a pound or two of glitter
But all I found was rotten milk
And a scent of reindeer litter

I didn't hear laughter or giggling
There was no music or sound
It wasn't long after starting
Signs of a struggle I found

The trail of bright red icing
Looked eerily like a sugary blood
And the brown mush that lay all around
Like smooshed cookie as thick as mud

I saw evidence of a bright, shiny button
And the most adorable green bowtie
And I knew without as much as a question
I smelled ginger but didn't know why

All of a sudden it hit me
I knew just what was wrong
It was right there in front of me
It had been there all along

This man with the image of goodness

I had become such a fan
But look out for our sweet, jolly Santa
For he ate the Gingerbread Man

Unknown
By Karen Schmidt

I've been to the place of unknown
And had to stay there for a while.
It seeped into my being, my bones,
And stole my willing smile.
It was blank and unrevealing
As I struggled to find there
In the dark forbidding corners
Answers to my prayer.
As I looked a shaft of light
Came shining through the gloom
The darkness of the unknown fled
It seemed a different room.
I reveled in that shaft of light,
It seeped into my being, my bones.
It brought the peace of understanding
And showed me what was known.
God is a tender, merciful Father
And trusting Him brings peace.
The hand that was nailed to the cross for me
Has a love that will never cease.
As that thought washed over me
It brought a sweet release.
One nail scarred hand held the unknown,
The other, laid over me, brought peace.

EERIE TALES

Here for your consideration, we have Eerie Tales. A collection of Horror fiction literature, with its roots firmly set in folklore and religion, its focus on the supernatural, demonic, death and afterlife, is played out here all in fun. These tales are both beautifully horrific and grotesquely attractive. Some are penned to test your comprehension of what you think is real, others paint and imagery that you hope isn't.

A startled reaction is the intention here, which purposefully creates an unsettling ambience. Here we strive to introduce our audience to a fascinating genre in an atmosphere of education and entertainment.

To quote H.P Lovecraft, "The oldest and strongest emotion of mankind is fear, and the oldest and strongest kind of fear is fear of the unknown."

So with this being said, we hope you will read these with an open mind, fluffy covers and of course don't forget a night light.

They're There Mother
By D.B. Martin

She had killed them. She had killed them both. She had held their small flailing frames beneath the water until they became still and neither float nor sank. Caught within the weightlessness limbo of the surface and the murky bottom of the lake. Then she had walked away and left them there. There had been no conflict and it hadn't been done in a moment of anger, no, it was purposeful. Yes, purposeful. They were her children, but she just wanted them gone. She just wanted to be free of them, to start life anew. Free from the bonds of motherhood and the responsibilities. Little Mary had been seven at the time and Jacob had been only three. They had both loved and trusted their mother unconditionally as children will. So when she had lead Mary by the hand and carried little Jacob down the boat ramp and out into the water that night they didn't even think to question her, they were with their mother.

That happened many years ago, for now she was on death row alone, for the past nineteen years. Now she wanted her children back. She wanted to show everyone they were wrong. She had never been able to convince herself they were really dead, that the things people were saying and had said that she had done were real. To her it had to be some sort of mass conspiracy against her. That is why she pleaded not guilty at the trial. The problem was that no matter how much she tried to convince herself and others of her innocence, she had been ultimately found guilty of murder, and was sentenced to death. She just knew that if she could get out of here, then she could find them, she could, she knew it. This amalgamation of the reality she sat in and the delusional dream she had constructed is oddly what held her together, and she awaited the outcome.

Then it came, today was the day. The day she had been excited about and afraid of all at the same time. Two burly guards entered her cell, sat her down and began cutting off her hair with oversized scissors. She said nothing. She just stared blankly forward, watching as the strands of silvery hair fell in front of her, feeling them softly land upon her lap. She just kept thinking that when she got to hell, God would know that she hadn't done this horrible thing and would take her to heaven. Then the guards began to roughly shave her head, still she uttered not a word. Once completed they walked her down a long, long hall, newly adored the chains around her ankles clanged against the hard concrete as she took each and every step and her hands were shackled firmly in front of her. There at the end of the hall, she could see there was door sitting open. Two guards with masks stood as sentries on each side, their eyes glowing within the sewn holes of the black fabric. She never faltered, not once. Boldly she walked in staring at the archaic looking wooden chair centered within the room. One of the guards turned her slowly, and she found herself staring into a mirror. Obviously a two way, so those who accused her could see her without having to actually face her. One of the masked guards knelt and removed the shackles from her hands and feet, then sat her down in the chair. He then began to re-shackle her hands to the armrests. The other guard placed a wet sponge on her now clean shaven head, then trapped it between her and a copper helmet he placed on top. The water ran down into her eyes as he tightened the helmet to her, but she never even blinked. Then once she was bound tightly they both moved back where she could see them in front of her. One asked if she wanted to say anything. She looked at him and said "I want to find my children."

The guards then moved out of her sight and she heard the word "Ready," Then the lights went dark. She felt an intense pain run through the course of her. Then it was quiet and there was nothing. Then a shaft of light came down from above her brilliant, and bright, turning on its own axis working its way toward her. She then felt as though she were rising, higher and higher, as if she were weightless. She heard music playing, beautiful music. Then it was quiet again. She found herself standing alone, everything was without form and white around her and beautiful. Then something caught her eye, it seemed to be coming toward her she couldn't make it out at first, then she realized it was man. She touched her head and realized her hair was back her beautiful hair and she knew, she knew this must be heaven. She had been taken to heaven! She was right and she ran toward the figure, then stopped just before she got to him.

"Thank you lord she said."

"What is your wish?" he asked."

"My wish?" she answered. "I want to find my children."

"Then go, go my child, look for them and know, on the day that you find them you may return."

"Thank you lord, thank you."

Then within a flash she found herself standing waist deep in water. She reached down and touched the cold liquid as she looked around. She knew this place. Why, she was on the old boat ramp, the very place where her whole nightmare had begun, she looked all around and she called out.

"Mary, Mary, Jacob, it's mother, come to me."

"Mary, Mary, Jacob, it's mother, come to me."

The Lord sat on his throne and gazed down upon her, watching her from heaven as Mary and Jacob played beside him.

Shadows
By D.B. Martin

It was warm under there, eyes shut tight, breathing in his own hot moist respiration over and over as he clung tightly to the edging of the thick cloth. He shook and his heart beat uncontrollably through every pore of his being. He didn't care though, not in the least because here, he couldn't see it. No, not here, not beneath the blanket. Here, somehow, he was safe. He knew it didn't make any sense, but it worked. As long as it worked it would be his sanctuary. It was a nightly ritual: the run. The run from the hallway to the warm bedding, but he knew, he just knew someday he wouldn't make it.

He was christened Joshua David and was born nine pounds and seven ounces, not a small baby by any sense of the word. Once he reached age three, things changed. From that point forward he became a slight sallow child, even bedridden for a while. Now he was continually cursed with insomnia and night terrors to the point that he remained sickly. He was a good child, though, and never gave his parents a word of trouble except at night. Every night when nine o'clock came, he was again ordered into the room, and every night in vain he fought them on this prospect. He had told them a hundred times why, but they never believed him nor even seemed to care. After a short while, they insisted it was just a childlike ploy to stay up for a little longer, but it wasn't.

Just because you don't believe in something, doesn't mean it's not real. It was there, there in the corner of his room. It was always there. If you walked past it, you may never see it. If you were not listening just right, you may never hear it. It was there just the same. If you looked just right and had your mindset tuned just so, then it all became horribly visible. Once it was visible, it was always there with its constant moans and cries, its strange human-like movements visible one moment then lost within the shadows of the room the next. This faint twilight apparition moved, huddling in the corners of his room, waiting, just waiting.

What was it was waiting for. Why didn't it just do whatever it was going to do and be done with it?

This worry and constant stress of the unknown weighed heavily upon him every night. Joshua would hum, sing loudly or recite sweet stories to himself, trying anything in insufferable vain attempts to drown out the sounds and formations of mental objects that choked his thoughts.

Joshua lay there, nested in his sanctuary again, listening to the crying, eyes peering just above the hemline of the blanket. He watched the shadow in the corner as it writhed and pulled, trying, it seemed, to get tighter into the corner.

"What do you want?" Joshua screamed out, but there was no reply. There was just the consistent crying and sorrowing. He couldn't take it anymore, no, not another night, no more. Joshua tore the covers back and leapt from the bed, now mere feet from this horrific vision.

"What do you want?" he screamed a second time. He took a single step forward, and the shadow twisted and rose, in and out, fading and forming. The moans and cries seemed to grow louder and louder.

"What do you want from me?" Joshua pleaded. "Answer me!" he said reaching out in an attempt to grab the faded form.

The Shadow then rose and fell, pulling itself tighter to the wall, suddenly within the grey, eyes open wide and staring.

"No!" it screamed, "Go away! You're not real! Go away, ghost. Go away."

"Ghost?" Joshua said, "Ghost?" He looked down at his hands and body which were almost formless like a shadow in the night, and he screamed!

Slatwood Box
By D.B. Martin

Beneath the moon, beneath the stars and far below the ringing bells and gargoyle grins of Notre dame. There lies within the catacombs that twist and turn beneath the arch of triumph, buried deep beneath the Paris streets and far below the cities lights an old slat-wood box. It is long forgotten by all that knew except by the one that mew. She was but small in frame, a fragile thing way too thin for life. She carefully lay her patchwork fur within the confines of the little box there among the dusty bone lined walls and patiently waited for what was to come. Life or death, which one would win she did not know for she was weak in body but strong in heart.

Her life had once been filled with dreams. She had not so long ago lived within a noble house. Her days were spent in the arms of a loving child and his family, and her nights were warm and dry upon a downed feather bed. Her food was served in crystal bowls and with all of this including love there was nothing more she needed. Her life was good and filled with purpose as every life should be. Her job had been an important one, and she had done it with unconditional love and pride. She would wake the house each morning so the family could start their day. She guarded the house through the day. She would then leave each day through the door her family made for her and walk along the broom swept streets to meet the child from school. Then safely guide him home again. Then each and every night she would lay upon her feathered bed and watch the child to sleep. Her life was content, her days complete and everything was grand. Then there came a day unlike any other. She walked the streets as times before to meet the little child but he was not there waiting. So faithfully, she sat and waited the remainder of the day, then finally when day was gone she went home alone. She lay upon her feather bed and waited for the child to appear. But when she woke from a fitful sleep he was still not there.

Then there came a bustling in her house, for several days on end. People screaming, people crying, and the child was still not home. Then one morning flowers came in boxes, flowers came in bunches, all the hours of the day, then as the day came to an end they carried in and lay a little box out upon the table within the window's bay. Cautiously she crept up close. Cautiously, she smelled. She jumped up to look inside and saw the little one lying there. Gently she climbed inside the little box and lay upon the child, sweetly rubbing his face with hers to say how she loved him so. Then the mother screamed and cried, "Get her out of there.

"Oh my god," she screamed as they grabbed her quick and threw her out the front door onto the pavement below. She dropped her head, they blamed me, she thought, for not showing him the way home. Maybe she was late that day, and maybe they were right to blame?

So she left the safety of her home and walked the savage streets. No longer did they seem so clean no longer did the world seem so right. Weeks had passed, but still the tears came each and every day. She missed the child, she missed her home, and she missed the family that she had. She was now on her own and all alone and her life it came apart. Her life was sad. She had no purpose, no love, or any sense of responsibility. So there she lay, frailty abound, exposed within the little slat-wood box there in the darkness of the catacombs. She lay there purring, dreaming of lovely times. Then she gently closed her weary eyes and released her final breath, there came a light within the darkness and shined upon the child's face smiling as he lifted her from the slat-wood box and held her close and tight.

Et Tu
By Paul Moses

He daubed the nape of his neck as he ascended the front steps, grumbling to himself: Hot for March. He hated hot weather, especially when he was out on a campaign in some sweltering, waterless wasteland (which seemed to be about half the time these days; so many rebels, so little time). The heat always made him itch under his armor somewhere he couldn't scratch with dignified propriety. Though by this time he fully considered himself to be a god, he was having an embarrassing difficulty controlling the weather, an annoying fact that his equally annoying wife had just pointed out that morning over cheese, bread and passion fruit (he made a mental note to give her a proper thrashing after dinner).

At least he was in Rome today. Hot or not, it was home. He hurried into the columned coolness of the senate building, ignoring the groveling obsequiousness of everyone he passed: "Your majesty!"

The bowing.

The knobby knees clunking on the pavement stones.

The prostration.

The averting of unworthy eyes.

It was both irritating and a little titillating, this business of being worshipped. A god's work was never done. Sigh. His favorite appellation was "Your Excellency"—such a nice regal ring to it—and several sniveling, genuflecting groupies warbled out the term as he passed. One was honored by having his hand painfully tread upon by the royal foot, snapping a pinky. A grimacing voice said, "Thank you, Your Excellency!"

As he trudged down the wide, polished corridor, he ran through his mental "to do" list. He wanted to get the day's work done as soon as possible and hit the baths. A brisk shampooing. A massage. Some vapors. A nice oiling and scraping. That's the ticket! Maybe a quick tussle with some plump little slave-girl.

But business first. There was the proclamation to deliver to the senate. A speech to make. I will be magnificent. A few cases to decide at court. Doubtless, some floggings to order. If all went well, a hanging or two. Then—to the baths!

He reached the top of the broad staircase that lead down to the well of the senate. He stopped and observed the room below. It was crowded today. They must be eager to hear my oration. The room was a churning mass of brilliant white togas, each one sashed diagonally with senatorial purple. These men always struck him as ridiculous—great, grasping clusters of power-crazed idiots. Apes in a zoo, scrambling for nuts. All the same. Greedy. Dissatisfied. Questioning. Criticizing his decisions. All clawing and moronic.

He smiled as he thought of how easily he had manipulated these men for so many years. They had once wielded the power of the state. But slowly, slowly, he had maneuvered and planned and fought and killed. Bribed and back-stabbed. Now he controlled the state. I AM the state! They prided themselves with being senators. But what was a senator? To him, they were no better than peasants. Despite all their vaunted power, it was he that they all called "Your Excellency".

His eye caught something below. A person. Someone who didn't belong. On the other side of the well of the senate, among the swirl-tide of white and purple, stood a tall, angular figure, cloaked in elegant, billowing black robes. Despite the stranger's height—a head higher than all around—and a ghostly pallor and an astonishing profusion of raven-feathered hair sweeping upwards, no one seemed to be paying him any mind. It was as if he wasn't really there. I must know who this is. But then a voice from the crowd:

"Hail, Caesar!"

Every head turned and every chin tilted up. And every voice, together, shouted, "Hail, Caesar!" This was the usual greeting, the standard salute, but today it was different somehow. It rang false, falling on the emperor's ears with an odd sensation. It had an unsettling dissonance to it. Too enthusiastic. Forced. Tinny. Sarcastic. A slight chill ran up the imperial spine.

The senate seemed to hold its breath as Gaius, Brutus and several other senators climbed the steps, hands held out in greeting. Gaius said, smiling like a chariot salesman, "Your Excellency! So good of you to come."

Caesar nodded, frowning slightly. Brutus said, "You honor us with your presence, my lord." Caesar pursed his lips in an abortive attempt at a smile.

Gaius said, "The senate stands ready to receive your royal proclamation, Your Excellency." The emperor held out his hand and his servant placed a scroll in it. With a cold, formal nod, Caesar handed the scroll to Gaius, who took it with a flourish of his bejeweled fingers.

Then Caesar saw the tall, black-clad figure again, this time in the middle of the crowd of senators. The man was moving through the crush effortlessly, as if not touching anyone. As he came closer, Caesar became terrified by the sight of his eyes—ebony orbs, oily, lightless. Those eyes were looking at Caesar. And through Caesar.

"You there!" the emperor shouted, pointing a slightly trembling hand. "State your name!" The senators all looked around, mumbling excitedly. A short, fat man, blushing scarlet, said:

"Me, Your Excellency? I am Cassius…"

"Not you! Him!" He jabbed at the air with an accusing finger. "State your business, sir!"

The man did not state his business. Those eyes. The death-paleness of his countenance. He stood still and silent, shaking his head slowly. Waiting…

"You will answer your emperor, sir! I am Julius Caesar…!"

Then Caesar screamed. A hot pain pierced his ribs. Looking down, he saw a bloodstain spreading from a knife hilt in his side. He couldn't understand what was happening. The knife was held by a grinning Gaius, who twisted the blade and pulled it out. Laughing, Gaius said, "Hail…Caesar…"

The emperor swooned, stumbled, and then, to everyone's surprise, seemed to recover himself a bit and started to make a speech, clutching his side. The little cluster of senators around him gave him some room to work and listened attentively. Force of habit. It was only right, after all. Caesar outlined his legacy and moaned something about expanded boarders. The man in black rolled his eyes, raising the fine arch of his brows.

Then the emperor screamed again. Another senator, a fussy, short-fused gentleman who couldn't listen for one more second, had thrust in his knife. Caesar took in a deep breath, swayed and continued his oration. Now, something about higher taxes for the farmers and tax shelters for government officials. The man in black was whispering in several senators' ears and they began drawing out daggers and making their way toward the steps.

Right in the middle of a particularly eloquent phrase about proposed senatorial yachts, another blade flashed and blood splattered. Caesar groaned. More blades. And more. More. A crimson shower burst forth in every direction. The emperor groaned, collapsed and rolled all the way down the steps, spraying his life's blood as he went. A little beyond the bottom step, Caesar convulsed, gasping, gurgling. Gaius, Brutus and the other assassins came down to watch him die. Senators gathered around the expiring dictator, each one wishing that someone else would end this. Then Caesar gave a long, mournful moan and his whole body relaxed, seeming to shrink into the leaching pool of blood around him.

Gaius held up his stained dagger and shouted, "The emperor is…"

Brutus interrupted with: "…is still alive." And it was true. Caesar pushed himself up to a seated position. Then up on one knee. Then to his feet. Wobbly, but he was up. The whole room gasped. Caesar wiped one red hand across his forehead, swabbing away a soggy forelock. He staggered towards the center of the room, blind and delirious.

The man in black wagged his spiky head. Good heavens, people! You call THAT murder? I think not.

Caesar opened his mouth—a little red waterfall gushed out—and began mumbling about lavish retirement plans and Greek islands ripe for the picking. The stabbings recommenced. From all sides now. Frantic. Furious. Caesar spun around and around, arms in the air, as if doing some freakish tribal dance. Then he was down again. The senators, slump-shouldered and thoroughly bespattered, stood around him, panting and gritting their teeth. The man in black made a little clucking noise. Couldn't even one of you hit a vital organ? A major artery? He is a man, not a pin cushion.

Caesar oozed blood and spewed vermillion vomit. One last cough…then, nothing. Gaius paused, listening and watching…waiting. Then he raised his knife in the air and…Caesar sat up. The man in black looked away, twisting his lips in disgust.

Brutus bent down and asked, "A last word, my lord?" Julius Caesar looked into his old friend's face and said:

"Hey! You're standing on my foot!"

The man in black scowled. Well, THAT will need some editing.

Brutus plunged his knife into Caesar's back. The emperor howled and keeled over on his side. Brutus stood and shouted, "For the gods and the Republic!" The exhausted room erupted in cheers:

"The tyrant is dead!"

"Long live the Republic!"

"Down with the dictator!"

And many other popular socio-political slogans jumbled over each other in a fatigued crescendo of enthusiasm.

Then Caesar sat up again. He gave a hiccup and tried to mumble something about hard currency. The man in black was piqued. He glowered at Brutus. You cannot even stab a man in the back properly? And you call yourself a politician! He grasped Brutus's hand—the one with the knife in it—and guided it home. Like THIS!

And Caesar died.

For real.

Amateurs.

The man in black stood at the top of the marble staircase next to the disembodied, blinking, stammering former emperor. The staircase was red. The floor below was red. The senators were red. The crumpled, lifeless form of Julius Caesar was red. The man in black said, "It has always astounded me just how much blood is contained in the average human body. It really is quite remarkable, you know."

"Wh…What?" Caesar emerged from his mental fog and took notice of the man beside him. The man looked out the window towards the courtyard's sundial.

"Ah, yes. Right on time. I do love punctuality. But I was beginning to wonder…"

"Wh…What?"

"Your friends should stick to boring people to death with their speeches. They are no good with knives." He took hold of Caesar's elbow. "Now you must come with me, sir."

"Wh…Whaaa…What?"

"I must say, Julius, you have had your more articulate moments."

"Julius? D…Did you just call me 'Julius'?"

"That is your name, is it not? Now we must go…"

Caesar pulled his elbow away, defiant. "You called me 'Julius'? That is 'Your Majesty'!"

"Hmm. Not anymore." He cocked one eyebrow in icy contempt and took Caesar's arm in an iron grip, dragging him away.

"And just who are YOU?"

"You may call me 'Your Excellency'…Julius."

INSPIRATIONAL

"My soul thirsts for you…in this parched and weary land where there is no water." (Psalms 63:1, NIV). The psalmist makes it plain that this world is barren and will leave you in want. He does go on in this psalm to give the reader a blessing which creates a vision of hope and establishes a firm foundation to stand. The blessing which is given is not just optimistic words with no power behind them. These words are rooted in truth and given power and authority by God. Truth spoken into the life of a person is not just meant to be heard and resonate in the ear. Words like this are to be graciously received and will resonate within the whole being. It brings forth life and power which is expressed in the words and actions of the receiver. The inspiring words of the psalmist move the reader to live out and be all that God has created him to be.

The psalmist and the prophets are not the only people who have this ability. God has shared this power and authority with all of humanity, after all we do have the image of God on us. God has allowed us the power and authority to speak blessings and curses into the lives of people who are around us. Solomon pointed this out when he wrote, "Death and life are in the power of the tongue." (Proverbs 18:21, NASB) So, it is important to be mindful of what you say and write. "Gracious words are a honeycomb, sweet to the soul and healing to the bones." (Proverbs 16:24, NIV). You should strive to be a good steward of the power God has given "so that your words will be an encouragement to those who hear them." (Ephesians 4:29, NLT).

These are the words you will find in this chapter of the Calhoun Anthology. What the reader will receive are inspirational words which build up and encourage. It is my prayer you will be blessed by the inspirational stories on these pages. After reading these stories, you may be aspired to tell your own story and share the blessing with others. Blessings are not meant to be selfishly hoarded, because in doing so they will lose their power and meaning.

Do not think that you, the reader, is the only one who benefits from this endeavor. I have personally found the inspirational words I write have a way of restoring and energizing me. "A generous person will prosper; whoever refreshes others will be refreshed." (Proverbs 11:25, NASB) The blessings of God have a way of bring unity between people and binding them in one heart, one mind, and one Spirit, pointing all of us to our one Hope. You should share in the blessing as well and share the blessing which you receive and reciprocate this by sharing it with others.

Coloring Within the Lines
By Gene Magnicheri

The Sunday Morning Worship Service had just started, but we were still not completely settled into our seats. Although we were on time, the trip from the car to the sanctuary proved to be the most challenging part of the journey. Getting my kids headed in the same direction in a timely matter can be like herding cats, very difficult to do. Despite the challenges of the morning we did make it to our seats with minimal disruption.

While scanning the bulletin to make note of the morning's Scripture verses, I was also listening to the morning announcements, which were delivered by the lay speaker. My 13-year-old son, Sam, settled quietly into his seat. He was not particularly thrilled about having to get up so early to make the early morning service. He never really argued about coming, but I can always tell his heart was not in it. He might be more enthusiastic with church if he could come later in the day.

My daughter, Sophia, was going through the activity bag, which she had carefully chosen from the display at the entrance to the sanctuary. It was this difficult life choice that was part of the reason we did not make it to our seats on time. However, getting one of these bags has become the Sunday morning routine and everyone knows it is not wise to break the routine of a four-year-old.

The church provides these bags, which are full of a variety of things that will occupy a four-year-old little girl until children's church starts. Usually Sophia will ignore all of the toys and puzzles in the bag and go right for the brightly colored markers. She has a love for art and, as with any artist, has a great deal of preparation, which must be done before starting on her masterpiece. While I was not paying much attention to her this morning, her routine is always the same. She will diligently search out all the markers and crayons in the bag and organize them on the pew. Once she is satisfied she has all the necessary colors for her masterpiece, she will start coloring in the children's bulletin. This morning started out no different.

Sophia is a well-behaved little girl, especially in church. She enjoys church and is very attentive to the events in the service. She has a fond appreciation for music, especially the livelier contemporary songs. The joyous and energetic atmosphere of the sanctuary has always captivated her. Still, no matter what is going on, she always finds time to color.

As the speaker was finishing the morning announcements and there was a little break of silence in the air, there came a loud and stressful complaint from Sophia. "My marker won't work!" she cried. The disruption startled me and stunned most of those in the immediate area. Of course, my first thought was to silence her, but in the back of my mind, I know this disruption from my daughter had a lot of eyes on me to see how this crisis would be handled. Not to be thrown off balance by the apparent developing crisis, I looked at my daughter to see if I could quickly and quietly resolve the issue at hand. Being a father of four, I am a pro at handling these kind of emergency situations. I have rehearsed such dramatic scenes in my mind so I would be properly prepared in the time of need.

As I calmly looked at my daughter and took a quick assessment of the situation, I noticed she was holding a bright blue marker. As I turned my gaze to her face, I could see the anguish the situation was causing her. Being oblivious to everything else going on around her, she continues her desperate cry, "And it is the blue one too. My favorite color." Apparently, the previous user of this particular activity bag had carelessly left the top off the marker and it had dried up. This was a major crisis because Sophia takes her art very seriously and she could not see the point of continuing without her favorite color. This situation was obviously going to put my crisis management skills to the test. This was a very serious situation and how I addressed it would determine whether we would be able to remain in the sanctuary or have to make a quick and unexpected exit so not to further disrupt the service.

In a whisper, I sympathetically told her I knew blue was her favorite color but the service had started and I could not get another blue marker right now. I reminded her she would be going to children's church in a few minutes and there were plenty of blue markers there for her to use. If she would kindly wait just a little longer, she would be able to finish her lovely picture then. She smiled and nodded her head in approval of my answer. Without another word, she picked out another marker and went back to coloring her picture. Another emergency averted!

As she went back to her work of art, my attention was drawn away from all the Sunday morning activities to a true artist at work as she carefully and skillfully filled in the outlined Biblical characters on her page. She was very careful to stay within the established boundaries on the page. I wondered who had taught her this. This was not something she had learned from me because I have been resistant to restricting her artistic ability with boundaries established by others. To work within predetermined limits, which had been created by outside influences, has always seemed prohibitive to me, especially when it comes to art. This does not mean I teach my children to live outside boundaries, but I do want them to feel free to question established boundaries so they will be able to come to a true understanding of why the rules have been put there to begin with.

As I watched her color, I was wondering what was going through her mind. I could tell with the intensity and care she was taking; her imagination was overflowing with ideas of what to do with this piece of paper. Even though the picture had boundaries and limits, it was not going to restrain her imagination or ability. It occurred to me those heavy dark lines, which outlined a picture, were just a guide for her to be able to express herself. Even the edge of the paper did not limit the full expression of this child as she colored. She was able to take what was given to her and create an expression of her soul within the borders and limits of a small piece of paper. It was from this creative representation of the soul being laid out on an 8 ½ x 11 page, I came to realize the lines were not restrictions or meant to restrain freedom of expression. She was viewing the lines on the paper as a promise and a guide. The lines were a guide meant to channel her ability with the promise of a real work of art. This was a collaboration between the one who created the lines and the one who colored the picture.

What had come to my mind while I watched this Master of the Crayola do her work was a verse from Psalm 119, "To all perfection I see a limit, but your commands are boundless." (Psalm 119:96, NIV) This was one of many verses I have remembered and reflected on frequently, mainly because I never understood what it meant. On the surface, this verse is confusing and is contrary to natural wisdom. What did the author mean he had seen a limit to all perfection? Even more puzzling to me was how could he see commands as being boundless? It would seem to me perfection would be without limits and God's commands were meant to set limits. I always felt there was more to this verse and this is the reason it had always stayed fresh on my mind. It took the demonstration of the joy and enthusiasm of a four-year-old little girl coloring a cartoon picture for this verse to open up to me.

What became clear to me from this art lesson was that joy, freedom, creativity and endless wonder can only be experienced within the boundaries of the law. Sophia's joy and enthusiasm in coloring within the lines, made me think of the words the psalmist used in his Psalm to God. A complete reading of Psalm 119 reveals a psalmist demonstrating the same joy, wonder and enthusiasm Sophia had for those heavy black lines on her paper. All throughout the verses of the psalm the author proclaims his delight and love for God's law. The Psalmist follows verse 96 by saying, "Oh, how I love Your law! It is my meditation all the day" (Psalms 119:97, NKJV). Overall in Psalm 119, "delight" for God's law is mentioned nine times and "love" for the law is mentioned nine times. It is obvious the psalmist did not view the law and commands of God as a restrictive edict, handed down from above. In the law, the psalmist saw the character of God and the love and care God had for him. The psalmist found blessing, hope, comfort, security, truth, wisdom, peace, and freedom in the law. Freedom was what the author alluded to in verse 96. It is in the fulfillment of the law he saw the freedom from sin and freedom to be what God had created him to be. The freedom from sin and freedom found in being what you were truly created to be is the boundless freedom the Psalmist was referring to. However, like all of those who lived before the coming of Jesus, he never did see the fulfillment of the law. He lived with the faith and hope of the One to come as being the Salvation for the world.

Jesus did come, and He was everything the Old Testament had promised Him to be. What were the hopes and prayers of the psalmist is now a reality for all of us. Those who believe and put their faith in Christ are not only forgiven of their sins, but are given a wise Counselor who will bring the life of Christ into their being (see John 14:26). Therefore, because I am a believer, I have the One who fulfilled the law living within me. This means the law, which I cannot fulfill on my own (Romans 3:23), is turned from a list of commands of what I should do into a list of promises of what I am becoming. This has become the reality of my life as I have seen my desires gradually change over time and I have realized the laws of God are not just stored in my head, but are also written on my heart and have become more evident in my life. I have become an "epistle of Christ…written not with ink but by the Spirit of the living God, not on tablets of stone but on tablets of flesh, that is, of the heart." (2 Corinthians 3:3, NKJV)

What I witnessed that Sunday morning was more than just a child who enjoyed coloring. What I had experienced was someone who had a deep appreciation for the finer things in life and who knew how life was meant to be lived. Life should be lived with a gracious appreciation for the rules and thankfulness for the boundaries, which have been set. Just as the boundaries of the shores have been set to contain the oceans and to protect the land, the law defines and protects our purposes in life. All of creation has to be seen in light of God's purposes in order to be understood. It is in His light we should live so that we will find understanding of the world. The ultimate experiences in life are found in the sacred and in our relationships. God demonstrates for us what is sacred and defines what life is to look like by His laws and commands, but it is only in my relationship with Christ is it possible to live this life out. It is my relationship with Christ where I find the freedom from the bondage of sin. It is by the power of the Holy Spirit working in me that I am becoming the image and likeness of Christ. It is by what Christ has done for me that I am able to look to an eternity of being exactly what God has created me to be. I will be perfect. . There is only one way to be perfect, yet in perfection there are endless ways of expression.. It is in the endless ways of expression that true freedom is experienced.

The other lesson learned in this art session was how important it is to be attentive to the small and simple things in life. While the sermon that morning was good and carried a powerful message, nothing could compare to the experience I had and the lesson I learned just from watching my daughter color. What is most amazing is it does not take years of theological training or understanding to learn this. When Jesus wanted to describe to the disciples what the kingdom of God looked like, He did not call on the religious leaders of the day as the example, He took a child. So, if there is a verse in the Bible which is giving you trouble or if you have some deep theological questions you need answers to, you just may want to buy a box of crayons and find a child to see what God may reveal to you.

April's Fool
By Gene Magnicheri

April Fools' Day is one of those times when I am on high alert. I have an alarm set on my phone to go off several times on that day to remind me it is April Fools' Day. I do this with the hope of not becoming the victim of some joker who loves to play tricks on people. I have this fear of being the featured movie on YouTube because of falling into the trap of a cunning prankster. I really do despise this day.

I have often wondered what genius thought this day up. It had to be the invention of some deprived mind. Or better yet, just maybe it was to celebrate the life of some man many years ago who had the undistinguishing repetition of pulling off the most masterful pranks. Either way, it is not funny. To find out who the culprit was, I decided to hit the Internet and see who was responsible for this dreadful day.

I found there are a number of theories on how this day found its beginnings. The one which I liked the most comes from an explanation provided by Joseph Boskin, a professor of history at Boston University. He said this all started during the reign of Constantine when the court jesters and fools told the emperor they could do a better job managing the empire. Constantine must have had a sense of humor as well, because he allowed a jester by the name of Kugel to be king for one day. Kugel was an opportunist and saw his chance to establish a day of fun and silliness. Being the king gave him the power to pass such an edict and the rest is now history.

Professor Boskin goes on to say, "In a way, it was a very serious day. In those times fools were really wise men. It was the role of jesters to put things in perspective with humor."

Out of all the different theories and explanations of the origin of April Fools' day, this one meets my approval. Here we have an account given to us by a history professor from Boston University. In 1983, the AP had picked this story and it was printed in many newspapers across the country. The only problem with the story was, it is not true, and that is why I love it. It is an April Fools' joke about April Fools' Day. You have to see the humor and the irony in that.

I, however, do have another theory about April Fools' Day. Keep in mind, this is just a theory, but I have very plausible evidence this is true. It is my personal opinion the very first April Fool's day took place in a garden called Eden. The prankster was a creature called Satan, who was in disguise as a serpent. The prank revolved around getting the two occupants of the garden to believe a lie.

The occupants of the Garden had been given everything which was needed for their pleasure and comfort. The beauty and the tranquility of having the perfect garden where there was no struggle or frustration is what humanity strives and longs for today. This garden was a place where all living creatures were at peace with one another. And of course, the greatest reward of all was fellowship with God. Life in the garden was simple and perfect. All they needed to do was to maintain the garden and enjoy the fellowship of God. The only rule given to them was not to eat of the Tree of Knowledge of Good and Evil.

Here is the trick. Satan was able to take the one thing Adam and Eve were forbidden to have and turn it into a desire. In fact, the desire became so great, they traded paradise for it. They traded in everything for nothing. Once Satan got them to desire what they did not have, and really did not want, it was all over. Satan was easily able to talk them into this, because at this point, they were only hearing and believing what would help them in obtaining the desire of their heart—the fruit of the Tree of Knowledge of Good and Evil.

So, what is the moral of the story? Stay away from talking snakes! That is a given. I prefer to stay away from all snakes, period, talking or non-talking. But there is another lesson here. We are still living out April Fools' Day. I cannot begin to tell you how many times I have traded the gift God has given me for a lie. I continually hold on to my life, not giving all to Jesus, thinking that I can somehow find peace, joy, and freedom on my own. I was not made to live on my own, therefore I will never be able to fulfill what I was created to be without God. Yet we are continually drawn into believing the lie that just maybe we can do this without God.

So, in reality, April Fools' Day does not come only one day a year. It comes every day for those who believe they can find their own fulfillment and joy apart from God. God did provide another way for man. A way that will do away with April Fools' Day forever. Two thousand years ago the Word became flesh and lived the life that we should be able to live, but cannot because of sin.

Even greater still, He was punished and withstood the full wrath of God that every sinner, who tries to stand on his own, will face. It is by His life, death and resurrection that I can stop being the fool and become the child of the King. I will never again be an April Fool.

You Are God's Poem
By Gene Magnicheri

Dear Daughter,

  I am so proud of you and absolutely love the young lady you have come to be. You have so much going for you and I want you to get the most out of life. The way to ensure that you will live life to the fullest is to look to the Author of life and seek His direction. God has created you to have a full and purposeful life.

  "For we are His workmanship, created in Christ Jesus for good works, which God prepared beforehand that we should walk in them." (Ephesians 2:10, NKJV) The word "workmanship" is translated from the Greek word "poeima." Poeima is where we get the English word poem. A poem is more than just a cute group of rhyming words. A poem is an expression of the author who is creating a work which is a reflection of who he is. It is the mirror into the heart, soul and mind of the craftsman as he pours all he is into his creation. It is truly a labor of love which reveals the character of the author and is expressed for all the world to witness and experience. You were made by God, for God and in His likeness. All of who you are and every little detail of your life has been shaped and designed thoughtfully and lovingly by God. You are a magnificent, beautiful poem created by the Great Author. Seek God's direction so you will live out and express all that God has created you to be. That is the secret to a happy and fulfilling life.

  Love,
  Dad

Finish the Race
By Millicent Flake

Therefore, since we are surrounded by such a great cloud of witnesses, let us throw off everything that hinders and the sin that so easily entangles. And let us run with perseverance the race marked out for us, fixing our eyes on Jesus, the pioneer and perfecter of faith. For the joy set before him he endured the cross, scorning its shame, and sat down at the right hand of the throne of God. Consider him who endured such opposition from sinners, so that you will not grow weary and lose heart.
Hebrews 12:1-3 (New International Translation)

This year marked my 12th running of the July 4th Peachtree Road Race in Atlanta, billed as the world's largest 10K. Over 60,000 people run and walk the course, with thousands of spectators lined up to cheer on the wheelchair participants and runners. I love the party atmosphere, the bands, the noise, people dressed up in costumes and folks out enjoying the day with their dogs and children. It's my favorite race of the year.

I'm always thankful that I am healthy enough to be there, that my legs are strong and my aging body can still make the 6.2 mile run. Each year as I make my way down Peachtree Road towards the finish at Piedmont Park, I'm thinking and praying for my loved ones struggling with their health.

This year I had my Aunt Beth on my heart. Beth was coming up on the end of her race, dealing with lung cancer that the doctors said would take her life. At 86, she was ready to go, but dying sometimes takes a long time, and she kept on going, slowly declining.

Aunt Beth and I had some discussions about what it would be like at the end for her, and the bottom line was that neither of us knew for sure. We knew what the Bible says, and that she was promised eternal life, but what would it be like when the final moment came? I couldn't answer those questions for her. Dying is ultimately a personal journey.

As I was thinking about these things I began seeing the Peachtree Race as a microcosm of life. Starting out under the huge flag that marks the beginning, everyone is happy and excited. Like children, we laugh and dance and bounce around on our toes, anxious to get going. As we finally begin, we all move together in one giant pack, this stream of people of different ability levels surging down the street. We trot along, each one finding his or her own rhythm, each picking out a course to run. Peering ahead, all I can see is the crowd, but when I look around me, I see open asphalt and room to run my race. I just need to keep moving forward at my own pace, not worrying if others are passing me. Isn't life like that as we struggle through our growing up years, finding our way and a place that feels comfortable?

Sometimes we meet people along the way, like my friend who was walking this year due to a bad knee and went most of the way with a young pregnant woman. Other times we have brief encounters, like when I fist-bump the Shepherd Spinal Center patients that line Heartbreak Hill in their wheelchairs. Some runners like to keep to themselves, while others prefer to have a best friend or family member running alongside them. Either way we are surrounded by others, encouraging us and taking our minds off of the discomfort we are feeling. Just as in life, we need others around for support, but we each have to keep our legs moving on our own.

Along the way I get tired. The downhill parts are fun, but going uphill is challenging, just as in life. I have to slow down, take some water breaks and walk a little. Sometimes if I'm too focused on my running I miss the fun all around me, the music and signs and outlandish costumes. I have to remember that I'm here to enjoy the race, not just get to the finish.

Finally, I'm getting close to the end, but the last mile always seems long. The crowds get bigger and louder, but my breathing is labored and I'm ready for it to be over. As the last half mile approaches, I find myself in the "zone" where all I'm focused on is seeing the finish line. The people around me recede into the background as I use the last of my energy to make it to the end. And then as I make one more turn I see the finish line ahead, and I know I'm going to make it. I'm going to finish, get my bottle of water and my coveted shirt and celebrate with my friends.

As I finish the Peachtree I often think about the passage in Hebrews 12:1-3, which compares our life to the end of a race. The writer envisions all the great "finishers of the faith" who came before us up in the stands of the arena, our "cloud of witnesses" cheering us on. I imagine my heavenly cheering section, including my parents, sister, grandparents, aunts and uncles, even my faithful pets who have passed on. Jesus is with them too. I see them clapping for me, the dogs barking, pride on every face.

I saw Aunt Beth getting more focused as she neared her finish line. Those of us with her along the way could only make sure she was comfortable and had what she needed, but she had to go that last mile by herself. She had spent her whole life training for this, and I was confident she would arrive with flying colors. But we couldn't do it for her. As she made that last turn, and finally crossed the finish line on September 15, I know her cheering section was welcoming her with open arms!

Unconditional Love
By Brian Grogan

When I pass from this world into the clarity of the beauty and purity of God's love, the dust of this world will no longer be beneath my feet. The seeds of God's love I leave in those whose hearts I am given the honor of sowing, will in time be a fertile land of Gods giving. May you all be greatly blessed.

The only hand of man who has true authority to reach into another's heart is its barrier for as much as we may try; the only person whose actions and reactions we can honestly control is our own. Any other is simply an illusion of our own ego. Today I freely give God my heart that it might learn to be truly free and happy thru the love of God that He grows there.

How beautiful the heart that gives love without regard of what the hand of man has given to them or expects to get in return for within them rest the wisdom of what brings true happiness for thy have tapped into what the hand of God has created us all to be and have realized how put the value of the dusty works of man put him in its place.

God loves us without condition and yet there are so many times our plans seem to have unexpected wrenches thrown in. The wisdom of faith in God tells us; even those wrenches are tools that the hand of God uses to fix unforeseen problems. If we choose to see them as such we will find the outcome is often better than we could have ever imagined.

What temporal eyes of man whose heart seeks to satisfy the ever elusive desire of the flesh? Any that was thought to satisfy it, blows thru one's finger as dust. The only true quenching of thirst that can be satisfied comes from seeking to express what love of God we can find in our hearts to whomever comes our way.

True freedom and happiness in this life comes not from the bloodshed and suffering of others but from recognizing the key that can only be found in letting God grow love in our hearts without regard to religion, color or language. The dust that He created us all from was as one in His hand. He formed and breathed his life in us that we may see to create suffering in another is to create it in ourselves. To express love to another is to show God's love and compassion on ourselves.

I once tried with all that I could muster to be a good person to no avail, in truth the lens I was looking thru was short sighted, and I had no memory of my pain. When I got to a point where I could take it no more I prayed so intently for God to change whatever it was I knew not how to and in return He showed me how He had planted a garden of love and hope within me in the decomposed suffering of my past so I could understand I had not had the pain, I could not truly appreciate the freedom of His love that lives within me.

Renewed Beginnings
By Brian Grogan

When I was a boy, I lived in a small southern town. It was 1963 and I was playing in the sand box in the backyard of my family's home...little did I know I was about to have my first real encounter that I remember with God the creator who I in time I would simply refer to as the God of unconditional love.

I remember the kindness and compassion I felt from the voice that I knew cared for more than even my Parents knew how. I felt it compelling me to push my little fist into the construction sand whose outside layer had hardened after the rain and I noticed the outside had not expanded and I felt God's presence revealing to me that the pile was mostly empty space and that all things in creation were merely an illusion,

I later came to understand that in life, that was how atoms worked and God explained to me that the energy within all things is in truth the breath of God that holds all things together. None of these things was widely understood in the small town where I grew up. Being able to hear from God in such a way hasn't made life as easy as one might think for the strength of faith must be cultivated over time and grown much as any other healthy and productive thing.

In 1966, I after being diagnosed with dyslexia, the so-called experts of the day said I would never be able to read or write well or take care of myself. As a result, I spent a lot my childhood years isolated, withdrawn and lonely.

Soon after I found an older youth that I thought was to be my friend. As it played out, he intended to take my child hood innocence away from me. I had a sheltered life in the era where I lived in. The only thing I knew of sex was how to spell it.

In time I found out I also discovered that I also had issues with traumatic memory loss and bipolar disorder and suffered for years from such memory's back that voice of God never completely left me and 12 years ago when I was 45 God had finally got me to a place where I could start using my past as something I could push away from as I learn a little better each day how to live and make decisions based spiritual principles which has taught that although one can never change the past. They can always learn to change their perspective of it and when they seek to be healthy, loving and giving without regard to who the receiver should be as we learn to trust God with those details then they will find true happiness and direction in life.

Paradox of Joy
By Marla Aycock

This beach scene *should* be littered with pieces of jagged broken glass, drenched with green bile, tears, and drops of blood— the water reflecting a face of desolate sorrows. Instead, eyes of joy, full of light are shimmering back at me. How can this be? The proof is before me as I look at the pictures taken during the third week of September 2013. There's a glow to my face, reflecting a peaceful presence, and yes—even laughter.

I remember looking in the mirror a mere six weeks earlier, my face frozen in a shroud of grief. I'd always been able to smile my way through most anything, but as I tried to lift the corners of my mouth, it was as if all memory of such an expression was forgotten. I literally could not smile without the aid of an index finger at each corner of my mouth. Even a hint of smile had been lost beneath the non-stop crashing waves of sadness and heartache.

From May 1, 2012 to August 1, 2013, exactly fifteen months, I'd endured a parent's worst nightmare. I watched the slow insidious enemy of cancer drain all the physical life out of my beautiful daughter, Esther.

I have a special relationship with each of my three daughters, yet each one is exceptional and unique. Esther was my youngest and she seemed to *get me* more than anyone else on the planet, creating a special deep bond. That alone made the sadness extra layers deep. The pain was multiplied a thousand times over because we were in a constant emotional wrestling match with her husband. The cancer was the easy part of the journey, and if you or a loved one has battled cancer, you know there is *no easy part* of cancer.

Even though the enormity of the *emotional battle* defies description, I find it necessary to give a short synopsis of its intensity. The overall significance of the day I'm about to describe makes more sense, and will have greater impact, when contrasted with the blackness of evil we experienced.

From the time we first met, the relationship between Esther's husband and our family was difficult. The 13 years' age difference, Russian culture, spiritual background, and intelligence training with the KGB...there were so many red flags. He *was* well educated, handsome, and physically fit. He had a love for music, art, and history which were real connection points for Esther. Daddies, however, know when it comes to their daughters and potential suitors; because they can read another man. Women rarely see the truth until it's too late. Esther's Dad, warned her from the beginning, "He's not who he seems."

Although there was much contention from her husband throughout Esther's illness, the last five months he began a campaign of lies, innuendo and character assassination against our family. When Esther went into a coma the last two weeks of her life we'd become aware of some specific malicious rumors he'd been spreading. During these last two weeks, our family was denied access to any medical updates. Lifelong friends disappeared or began treating us like enemies or lepers who had no right to be near our precious girl. We had to leave her bedside as she neared death to get some professional counsel as new lies and threats were brought against us which could have had dire consequences. We didn't get to be with her when she passed from this life. We were denied information as to where her body had been taken so we could say our final goodbyes. We still have no gravesite or urn of ashes to help us grieve. We took part in two different memorial services for her. The second one gave our extended family and close friends some healing and closure. So, with this short background in place, let's proceed to my *paradox* of *joy*. (A more complete story will be forthcoming in Esther's Memoir, "Supernaturally, Natural,"). *This* story's focus is *joy*.

Now, the corners of my mouth lift without effort at just *the thought* of sharing this one delightful day of healing with you. Without the previous backdrop of darkness and pain, I might have missed the beauty and brilliance of the Lord's loving grace right in front of me on Monday, September 16, 2013. I call it, "Miraculous Monday."

The necessary two memorial services we attended to honor Esther's life were behind us. My sister, Lanette, the guru of time-share vacations, gifted my daughter Kristi and I with a chick-week at the beach. Myrtle Beach, S. C. was a special place for Esther, where our family had made many precious memories.. We chose this location, but a different venue was selected to give some healing space for our tattered hearts.. The *important* thing to note, was Myrtle Beach was special to Esther.

Not just the beach was special…anything in nature renewed Esther. At her work place, colleagues would often tease her. If it was a nice day she'd go outside, unfurl a blanket in a shady spot, eat her lunch—and with a Cheshire cat smile, catch a quick nap. It was a healthy thing to do. After a while a co-worker or two would be enticed to join her. She had a gentle quiet influence over people. She drew them into her world without coercion.

In this love of nature, she and I were definitely kindred spirits. Often my outings with Esther were just a day trip to north Georgia. We'd find a location near a lake, river, or forest…spread out a blanket, and lay there *ooo-ing* and *aww-ing* over the beauty before us. Sometimes the beauty was in odd places. One time while exploring new vistas, we found a town with a cemetery on a hill overlooking the surrounding mountains. It offered a view of the quaint mountain village below us also. After a bit of poking around and exploring the graves, we found a large oak tree at the top of the hill…the perfect place to spread out Grandma's patchwork polyester quilt and devour our homemade lunches. We took turns reading a fascinating book to each other. It was a sweet renewing time for our souls.

Camping was also a great love of hers. I'd been there and done that, so I left her to her own *young* friends to enjoy God's wonders and the companions of heat, cold, bugs, frostbite and sleepless nights. Esther loved nature and everything about the outdoors reminds me of her. The significance of the day I'm about to describe encapsulates this love.

Strangely enough, Lanette, Kristi and I arrived at the resort on Friday the 13th of September, but bad luck was *not* on our radar. We had a gorgeous ocean-front condo on the fourteenth floor. Oh, the magic of a wide expanse of ocean and sky to help us breathe deep, and salty air to purify our body. The renewal began immediately. Standing on the balcony with eyes closed, arms open wide and breezes caressing my body, I had the euphoric sense of flying.

This resort just assigned a room when you arrived—no pre-choosing. So, our delight was pure thankfulness and praise for our Lord's gracious provision.

We settled in, and per our custom, we moved the coffee table to the ocean-view balcony and laid out our dinner complete with candles. A sweet joy settled over us as we began this week of healing our shared pain.

At the end of the meal, my sister handed me a gift. It was a book titled, "Tear Soup." Written in a child-like format with large artistic pictures and simple profound words, this thoughtful gift helped walk me through my first steps of healing. The simplicity of the book made it an easy read, and readily accessible to my grief-shattered heart. My sister is one of the most compassionate, giving people I know, and I'm so thankful she's family and always there for me.

Sunday, our second full day at the resort, seemed to be the day laughter returned to our lives. Late afternoon we decided to eat at Red Lobster. We arrived during the busy dinner hour and had to wait for a table, so decided to use the time to do a photo op. The timing was perfect. We had the blush of sun on our skin, makeup in place, three days of rest, the happy anticipation of yummy seafood, *and* perfect lighting. The pictures we took are still some of my all-time favorites.

We were finally settled at our table and the waitress gave us her spiel… "The margaritas are amazing, and tonight we have a special. You can order the next larger size for only a dollar more." Lanette and Kristi took the upgrade, a strawberry for Kristi and peach for Lanette. I'm a lightweight when it comes to alcohol, and planned to take only a sip of theirs. Well, they were not just a *little* larger, they were *mammoth-sized* margaritas. Just put your whole head in the glass and inhale, type margarita. I sipped far beyond my normal limit, and we returned to the resort a couple hours later with happy tummies and *feeling good.*

Our evening entertainment found us gathered around the dining room table to play a game of Farkle. "No," that is not a misspelled word, and "No," it's not a dirty word. Farkle is a dice game which is pretty much brainless as far as difficulty, but at the same time, gives plenty of opportunity for silliness and laughter—which we did in abundance. The deep belly laughs felt good and were so healing.

The weather had been perfect with glorious sunrises and magnificent sunsets. We eased into what would be called our *magical Monday,* and the weather did not disappoint. Early Monday morning, I glanced over the railing of our balcony…"Aha!" I spied a large swimming pool I hadn't noticed previously...perfect for swimming laps. It was 8 a.m., and with coffee and a muffin in hand, Lanette and I headed to the pool while Kristi went to the beach for a jog. As I swam there was a hint skittering the outer edges of my mind…just maybe, *life could be good again.* After a delightful time of exercise, we went back to our room and followed up with a Nutri-Bullet green drink. This was a very good habit formed while dealing with the extreme stress, and long days and nights of Esther's cancer care.

It was ocean time and we gathered all our beach gear including boogie boards, and headed down fourteen floors to claim our patch of sand for the day. "Yes!" I exclaim. "The waves were nice but gentler than yesterday." I was squashed like a bug by three big ones in a row. I forgot my reading glasses were still atop my head and they were swept out to sea to become *sea glass*, or for some far-sighted sea creature to make good use of. Lanette, not much for actually getting *in* the ocean, went for a walk on the beach while Kristi and I headed out to catch waves with our boogie boards.

Our family spent many years vacationing at Myrtle Beach in a camper and catching waves whether body surfing or on firm canvas rafts, it was a given…it's what we did. Boogie boards were actually an upgrade for us. We spent about thirty to forty minutes catching waves when I noticed it was raining both north and south of us. Not wanting our towels and beach gear to get wet, I said, "I think we'd better head in." Before we could make it to shore we started getting pelted, but managed to rescue most of our things and scurry to the overhang of a building to wait. It didn't last long, the sun popped back out, so we headed back to the beach to work on our tan.

We'd just settled in when I began to see fish jumping out of the water to my left not far from shore. (Being the nature lover that I am, in the past, I would have waded out to get a better look.) Experience and observation had taught me better. Now I know when fish jump out of the water at the ocean, there's usually a bigger fish feeding. In other words, *stay out of the water*. I thought it very strange as it was noon and not the usual time for fish to feed. Before long, *really big fish* started jumping out of the water. They were maybe forty to fifty feet from shore. My breath caught and heaved, as wide-eyed I screamed the word no one wants to hear at the ocean…especially if you're *in* the ocean. "Shaaarrrk!" Correction… "Shaaarrrks!" If I hadn't seen this with my own eyes, I wouldn't have believed it. I'd been going to the ocean for many years and never seen *one* shark jump out of the water, yet this turned into a circus of sharks. The activity was mind boggling. The sharks would attack the school of fish and like an explosion of dynamite, dozens of smaller fish would catapult several feet into the air. The sharks were leaping several feet out of the water, leaving no doubt regarding their identity. Quite a few people were in the water, so first we looked for the lifeguard who'd been high on his perch a few minutes earlier, but nowhere to be found now. We screamed at people to get out, but the roar of the ocean drowned out our voices. After several minutes the lifeguard finally showed up and blew his whistle to get people's attention and signal them in to shore. He hadn't even noticed the sharks until we told him. (This increased our confidence of safety with a lifeguard on duty...Not!)

It was a bit terrifying and exciting all at the same time. Terrifying, because Kristi and I had just been boogie boarding close to where they were feeding...and exciting because I love watching wild life and had never even seen such a mesmerizing scene. There must have been a *very large* school of fish to feed on as no one was harmed. The feeding frenzy went on for so long we got hungry too and went up to our room for lunch. When we looked out from our balcony they were still feeding which continued for at least an hour. Incredible!

After lunch we decided maybe it was time to go *inland* for some retail therapy. We'd enriched our tans and met our sun quota for the day and had a sudden *decrease* in our passion for boogie boarding.

The stores were stocked to the gills (pun intended) with new fashions so we went a little crazy for the next two to three hours ogling all the new styles, and taking load after load to the dressing rooms. We didn't buy much but we sure had a lot of fun, *giggly-girl moments,* which a man will never understand. My back started hurting so we went back to the condo. Too much boogie boarding in a *not-so-young-any-more* body I think.

My sister, Lanette, and daughter, Kristi, made dinner while I lingered out on the balcony for a bit. As I gazed out at the ocean, a lone dolphin swam up close to the shore, hesitated a moment, and then turned around and swam back out to sea. "Hmm...that was cool," I thought. It was a sweet moment and I felt like it was just for me. Although after the earlier shark extravaganza, it was a bit anticlimactic. Maybe it was just communicating..."stick around, you ain't seen nothin' yet!"

It seemed I no sooner stretched out on my bed to relax the muscles in my back, when I heard my daughter, Kristi, announce, "Supper's ready." I saw the meal being laid out on the balcony coffee table..."Yum-O!" I exclaim, "Taco Salad, one of my favorites." We sat down ready to dig in. Rumbling sounds began off in the distance. Very quickly the thunder became loud as it echoed between the condo towers. Sun bathers and beachcombers started scurrying toward safety. The thunder intensified and lightning began to flash. We looked over the balcony at our beach chairs and umbrella below where we'd left them for watching the sunset later. Because of the storm the tide was higher than usual and our gear was on the verge of being swept out to sea. We raced down to retrieve them as rain started falling hard and great flashes of lightning began striking…thinking, "We're crazy! Maybe we should just let the sea have them." The umbrella looked part sand castle and the chairs sediment encrusted. We quickly drug them to a sheltered area and left them. We'd come back later and give them a shower.

We made a hasty retreat and headed back to our room. Seated on the balcony once again we attempted to finish our supper. Thankful for our *cold* salad, but once again supper was put on hold. Out of the corner of my eye I saw a blinding flash of light. I looked and realized the sun was coming back out, yet we were still *watching the storm in front of us*. I jumped up and said, "There's going to be a rainbow!" (Rainbows were a special sign to Esther of God's promises to her and she experienced several full ones during her illness.) Lanette and I ran out of the room where we could see the western sky. The sun was out full. Just as I realized the rainbow would be in the east I started back toward the balcony when I heard Kristi cry out, "There's a rainbow right in front of me!" It was a half bow coming right out of the water. Then a double rainbow started forming and we started taking pictures like a paparazzi crew.

As the rainbow faded, I sat down to finally finish my supper and off to my right I started seeing black objects jumping out of the water. At first I thought the school of sharks were back. They were out a way, but then I saw the *clear* form of a dolphin jump out of the water. I grabbed the binoculars and as I looked, four dolphins jumped out of the water in unison. It looked like the beginning of a dolphin show at Seaworld. Then over a wide expanse of water, scores of dolphins began jumping out of the water in an amazing display of *joy* and *playfulness*. We watched for at least twenty to thirty minutes. What was happening? This was just crazy. In the past, I'd felt very blessed to see one small pod of dolphins passing by on their way to feed in the early morning or late afternoon hours.

When the show was over, I walked into the condo and exclaimed to my sister, "Oh my goodness, God sure outdid himself today!" Lanette agreed. Then there was just a sense of Esther's laughter as she could see I *got it*! She was up to the best kind of healing mischief she could have brought to my soul this day. I could imagine her in a conversation with Jesus making a *special request* to put on an extravaganza of joy which we couldn't miss. Or maybe it was His idea and a way to bless Esther's heart as she took part in it. Regardless, to me it felt very validating of God's love. You may think I'm crazy or at least grief-crazed, but there was just something too *supernatural* about it all to be humanly explained away as coincidence. The whole thing was so like Esther. Remembering how much the world of nature meant to her, all of the above was intertwined with the outdoors, her style of playfulness, and in a place she loved. It was such a gift.

But this day was not over yet…one more event sealed these God-designed supernatural moments for me. I went back out to the balcony and watched the last remnants of the rainbow fade. There was a white shimmering curtain of mist cascading into the ocean from the end of it. I was in awe of its beauty. Both Lanette and Kristi were on their cell phones absorbed in conversation. Unable to get their attention, I looked up and saw an amazing lone cloud. It was puffy and billowy reminding me of an exotic flower with a pretty coral-pink light glowing from the center. When I thought to take a picture, it had lost most of its color, but I wanted to remember every moment of this unique day. As the sun was setting I went back into the condo and brought the cloud picture up to view it. I almost dropped my phone because what I saw took my breath away. I let out a gasp of joyful delight, as Esther's face was in the cloud. I wasn't trying to see something, but…there it was…her sweet face peeking out of the center where the glowing coral color had been moments before. I laughed as tears flowed…let's just say it was a very emotional moment.

If you're familiar with the famous artist Bev Doolittle and her camouflage technique; her paintings are filled with detail where the real picture is hidden. Her painting called "Woodland Encounter," appears to be a forest of white birch trees, but hidden are several American Indians riding horses through the woods…their presence becomes more visible with the viewing. In the same way, I took a picture of a cloud, but hidden in it was Esther's face. It was meant as a special healing moment for me so it doesn't bother me if others can't see it. But, if you hold the picture about arm's length away and check out the flesh-colored center of the cloud, you can see her face peeking out. A ridge of her dark hair contrasts below the white cloud, her broad forehead with her eyes and nose below. Her chin and mouth are tucked into the lower part of the cloud.

Several days later I was showing the picture to my son-in-law, but what he saw was the large eye in the upper right corner of the picture. So maybe my impression of Esther and Jesus working together wasn't so far-fetched? Besides, if mere man can store his pictures in a cloud, why can't God?

This was my Magical Monday…and to me, it defies any other explanation other than God's tender love and mercy knitting this momma's shattered heart back together.
Psalms 57:10 "Your mercy and loving-kindness are great, reaching to the heavens, and your truth and faithfulness to the clouds."

A life lesson I've taken away from this day is… "Even this special day of joy wasn't possible without the storm." Look at the many elements of this one day…water, sand, sunlight, dark clouds, thunder, lightning, storms, inconvenience, peaceful moments, good food, interruptions, shopping, giggles, excitement, fear, revelation and yes, *joy*.

Our last night there, the last picture I took was one from our balcony of a full moon hanging in a dark velvet sky just above the horizon. As I looked at it, there was a thrill of delight as I saw the Lord's seal on this supernatural week. The light reflected off the moon in the perfect shape of a cross.

I'm presently working on Esther's memoir titled
"Supernaturally Natural"
by
Marla Aycock

Value of Society
By Karli Land

John 10:10 says *"The enemy does not come except to steal, to kill, and to destroy."*
What better way to attack a woman than to attack her self-worth?

I used to love getting magazines in the mail. I knew that once a month, Teen Bop was coming with a handsome boy on the front and a quiz inside that would tell me which *New Kid on the Block* member I was going to marry based on my responses to five questions. I may not have had much else to do that month but magazine day was blocked out on my calendar. I'd spend the entire day reading celebrity gossip and interviews, learn about the newest fashion no-no's, and read all about which acne products would work overnight.

I now have daughters at the magazine-reading age and it's terrifying. Magazines for teens are not what they used to be. The covers are filled with young girls with perfect skin and very little clothing. Quizzes now tell us if we are flirty enough to keep our man. Ads for diet pills litter the pages while articles explain why it is okay to hit on your best friend's boyfriend and teach the ins and outs of sexting.

Our children are growing up in a very different world. Society is full of lies that can defeat a girl using only the front cover of a magazine.

Society tells us we must be young.
Society tells us appearance is everything.
Society tells us we must attain an 'unattainable' body shape.
Society tells us social status matters.
Society tells us smarter is better.
Society tells us we only need worldly wisdom.
Society fills us with the idea that we have to be good enough to accomplish anything.

I don't know about you, but this shakes my faith. God tells me to do something but my mind tells me I haven't got what it takes.

Spend much time in the magazine aisle and you will leave feeling defeated. Imagine being a teenage girl living in today's ego-eccentric world of perfectly shaped models with flawless skin and hair which falls perfectly in place each and every morning. We all know that those ladies don't wake up that way but it still tears into our subconscious that we don't measure up. We start to look at the emphasis that is placed on the 'perfect' woman and we know that we aren't her.

We must fight those thoughts of worthlessness.

When the enemy says that beauty makes us worthy, remind him that Proverbs 31:30 says "Charm is deceitful, and beauty is vain, but a woman who fears the Lord is to be praised."

When the enemy says that you fall short of perfection, remind him that Psalm 139:14 says "I praise You because I am fearfully and wonderfully made. Wonderful are your works; my soul knows it well."

And when the enemy tells you that you are nothing but a sinner, remind him that Romans 5:8 says "But God demonstrated His love for us, in that while we were still sinners, Christ died for us."

Society isn't going to change. Our hearts must change. We must realize that beauty is not determined by our weight, our height, our social status, future achievements, or past failures. We are beautiful because of the image of Christ that is in us.

SHORT STORIES

When we think about short stories and attempt to define them, it gets boring. Most writers agree they need to be under 10,000 words, and have the same five elements of a novel; characters, setting, plot, conflict, plus a good theme are essential. Being able to finish it in one sitting is also a leading requirement among those that teach fictional writing. I like to think there's more.

My idea of the perfect short story definition comes from Stephen Vincent Benet. He said a short story should be read in an hour, and remembered for a lifetime.

Someday When I Get Old
By Mike Ragland

A couple of weeks ago, after volunteering at the museum I walked down to the end of Broad Street. After feasting on a Chicago dog at Roger's hot dog stand I was nearly back to where my car was parked when I saw this old man sitting on one of the benches at the corner of the block. He had to be at least eighty and was talking to a nicely dressed young man sitting next to him.

I sat down beside him to talk

As I got nearly even with them the old man lit a cigarette and the young man got up and walked away. Now my church does a street mission program and I have gotten familiar with a lot of the street people in town. But I didn't recognize this fellow. He had on a crumpled up shirt, a pair of dark colored pants that appeared to be clean with some built in stains. He hadn't shaved for a week or two and wore no socks with his worn out shoes. And lastly he was wearing a baseball cap of some kind that was so faded you couldn't read anything, but it looked like it might have been green at one time.

I thought to myself, oh boy, I'm going to get me a couple of good stories right here. You see I'm a sucker for old people, especially old men that have been around the mountain a few times. They all have good tales of life and lost loves with experiences to back them up. That's exactly the kind of stories that I want to be able to tell when I get to be an old man.

I sat down and attempted to strike up a conversation with the old fellow.

"Need any help?" I asked.

"Help?" he asked back. "I need my granddaughter to come and get me. I don't want to sit here all day."

I thought to myself. Yep, when I get to be an old man I'll be as stubborn as I want to be and won't listen to anybody.

He turned, looked at me and said. "Did you see that fellow that just left?"

"Well I just asked him what time it was and he got up and left. He had an ear-bob in his ear. Never trust a man with an ear-bob in his ear."

And when I get old, I thought, I ain't gonna trust nobody that ain't at least sixty-five.

I finally asked if he had any family other than the granddaughter he was waiting for.

"I had a whole house full of young'uns. My wife died over thirty-five years ago and I raised them all. Course they're gone now."

"So you never remarried?" I asked.

"When you got a house full of kids to raise, you ain't got time to hunt for a woman," he replied. "Look mister," he said, "I just come to town to straighten out the mess the VA has made of my check "I don't drink. I don't need much to live on. Women's what takes yore money, without them it ain't too hard to get by."

Finally, I got him on a roll. He told me all about his children, the ones that had been successful and the ones who hadn't. The ones who were having problems with alcohol and the ones who lived with him but left cause he played a lot of preaching on the TV.

His granddaughter pulled up and hollered. "Get in grand-paw we're going to be late."

He gave me a wave as he got in the car. I noticed he had a big smile on his face.

I sat there reflecting on what he had just told me. I doubted if I could get a story out of it, but I sure did envy him. I kept thinking, he doesn't care what anybody thinks, says what he wants to, and can be a stubborn old coot. The wrinkled shirt and baggy pants, shoes with no laces and feet with no socks also gave me the impression that dress was not a factor in his life.

I was basking in the sun when I was startled by a car horn. I think I might have actually dozed off and jumped a bit when the horn sounded. I looked up and there was my daughter and granddaughter sitting in her car at the traffic light. My granddaughter was frantically waving for me to come to the car. As I approached the car they both started yelling for me to get in. I crawled in the back seat and they pulled off.

"What's up?" I asked as we headed down Broad.

"What are you doing?" my daughter asked.

"Not much" I replied. "Just got off at the museum and was headed for my car at the parking deck. Why do you ask?"

"How long have you been sitting there?" my granddaughter asked.

"Didn't time it," I said. I was beginning to get skeptical at this line of questioning. And I once again asked why.

"Grandpa," said my granddaughter. "You're sitting out here on the street looking like that. You're lucky some church group didn't offer you a personal hygiene bag. And half the people in this town know who you are. What do you think was going thru their minds when they saw you sitting here?"

"Bekki," I said to my daughter. "What's she talking about?"

"Daddy, you're wearing men's shorts that look like they were wadded up in a ball and then you put them on, and the shirt you're wearing is frayed and faded and probably has a hole in it somewhere. And when's the last time you were at a barber shop to get your beard trimmed and shaped?"

"Is that all?" I asked. "Where ya'll going anyway?"

"We're going to the mall," my daughter said. "Where are you parked?"

"I'm in no hurry," I said. "I believe I'll go with ya'll."

"No you won't," my granddaughter said. "We're going to get something to eat first. And you've already eaten."

"How do you know that?" I asked.

"Cause part of it is still on your shirt. It looks like mustard."

I always do that I thought. I tried to get it off and then forgot about it.

"And grandpa," she continued, "You have several pairs of nice tennis shoes and dress shoes. Why do you insist on wearing those Jerusalem cruisers with no socks when you go to the museum?"

"Jurusa what?" I asked.

"Sandals, Daddy," my daughter answered.

"Well for one thing they're comfortable and I like 'em."

"And would it be too much trouble to get rid of that old faded out Alabama hat."

"I'm not going to get rid of my hat," I said. Then I added a "Roll Tide" just for good measure.

"Well could you at least get another one. Maybe a white one, so when it got dirty even you could tell it."

"Grandpa," Mattie said. "You can go with us if you really want to, but at the mall would you remain in the car."

"Nah, I'm going to walk real close to you and tell everybody you're my baby girl."

"Mama," she said.

"He's just being stubborn like always," my daughter said with a smile on her face.

They took me back to my car. When I got home I told my wife about all that had transpired.

She thought it was funny. I knew she would.

I sat on my back porch this past week-end remembering the old man. I wish I had gotten his name. Cause when I get to be an old man I'm going to act the same way.

"Martha, is John Hagee on yet?"

One for The Good Ol' Boys
By Mike Ragland

A few months back I wrote a blog about some Yankees coming through my little home town of Cave Spring. And while they were having breakfast in a local café near me they insulted the grits that was brought to them. Most folks thought the column was quite humorous and I received a lot of positive comments and emails that stated that fact. But not all of them did.

I received a comment from a lady in New England who was born and raised in the south. She stated that it was men like me that prompted her to move and I could take the grits and homemade Southern breakfast of biscuits, and Redeye gravy and stick them up my Rebel butt. Modern women had better things to do than get up, fix food, and be a waitress for some man who was no better than they were.

I e-mailed her back and apologized for being so crude in her eyes, but I would like to know a couple of things. I just wanted to make sure I understood what a modern woman was. I simply asked if she was married or had a boyfriend and did she shave her legs.

I can't put in print her reply, other than I was a Neanderthal and Mencken was right when he said the south was an intellectual Sahara. She advised me in no uncertain terms it was none of my business if she ever married or shaved her legs. And of course, she was right. But now I knew. She stated she enjoyed her life in the Green Mountains of Vermont where intellectual people lived and conversed.

I then tried to explain the cultural differences. For instance, Nascar made the "good ol' boys" quit bringing long necks to the race track. They were afraid somebody might insult the good name of Dale Earnhardt which was a sure fire way to get your head bashed.

And I couldn't apologize for country music. We loved Willy and Waylon—and if Gretchen Wilson didn't mind calling herself a Redneck woman, and wanted to leave her Christmas lights on her front porch all year long, that was her business. Preaching is on the TV somewhere twenty-four seven, and on another channel there are John Wayne re-runs. And about once a year we watch Gone with the Wind again hoping it will end differently.

She said she had retired to the North in her twenties because we were loud and boisterous. I think she was indicating we drink too much. I can't argue with that I said, we do like to tap our foot along with David Allen Coe and Loretta Lynn.

We also like to fish and hunt. I asked her if she knew how many good ol' boys it took to catch a Catfish. Four I replied. It takes one to catch the thing, another to write a song about it, and two to start a fist fight in the parking lot later arguing about how big it was.

And then there's football. I'll bet you don't like football at all do you. Well the good ol' boys certainly do. At last count I could only come up with nine professional teams in the South. But then there is the SEC, which includes Alabama and eleven other teams. And I can't forget about their little sisters in the ACC. So please give us our football Mrs. Vermont, a fellow can only fish and hunt so much you know.

That brings me back to what you said about Mencken. He made his statement without much investigation, and from Baltimore. It's not exactly Oxford or Cambridge, is it now?

I was stationed in Connecticut once upon a time. And on our first weekend of liberty we went to New York City, 'cause the drinking age was 18. It didn't take us long to find 42nd street and a place called the Peppermint lounge. Now this was in 1965 and things were different than today.

Across the street was a bar called the Club .45. We liked it a lot better than the Peppermint Lounge and got a table. Couldn't get to the packed bar. I finally said, "How about y'all letting a feller get him a beer, if'n you don't mind. "Things got quiet and some guy bought all of us a beer.

Our table was soon full of giggling yankee-girls. One of my buddies eventually married one of them. Anyway they wanted me to keep talking. I'd give them a lot of ain'ts and hain'ts and grey-its and tell them they was purtier than a whole litter of speckled puppies under a red wagon. And they just giggled and giggled. As I remember, they were right friendly girls.

That was a lesson well learned. I was in Connecticut for three months and never had to buy more than the first drink in any bar in New York if I'd lay on the Southern Accent. I was back in the city several years later and it still worked, wonder what Mencken would have thought of that.

Please understand that I wrote the blog about Cave Spring as a public service. I had just finished reading some stories by a famous Southern Philosopher named Jerry Clower. Now Jerry is of the opinion that if more women would get up in the morning and cook real biscuits, not "Whomp" biscuits that come from a can, it would cut the divorce rate to almost nothing.

One of my favorite Southern authors, the immortal Lewis Grizzard, was a little more forceful. He quoted his boyhood friend and idol, Weyman C. Wannamaker, a great American, on hairy legged women. Weyman had said that he wouldn't take a hairy legged woman to a rat killing.

My grandson while reading over my shoulder said that I should throw in a little Friedrich Nietzche or Jean-Paul Sartre and show the lady that we do have some education. He's a college boy and knows everything, so I did. But I told him he better warn those fellers that if they got around Talledega on race Day and started running off at the mouth some good ol' boy would bash their head in with a long neck. I guarantee it.

Focus
By Vickie McEntire

"Can you even hear what I'm saying?"

She begged to be understood. Her eyes stung. She pretended to shield the sun from her view as she pressed her eyelids shut with the tips of her fingers to prevent tears from exposing her pain. The camera weighed heavy in the grasp of her other hand.

"I'm trying to teach you, but you need the knowledge first. You think you can come out here and look through the viewfinder and just figure it out?"

Her husband was hot, tired, and frustrated. He had driven an hour, one way, to Chattanooga on three occasions in three days to chase the "money shot". He was now standing in the shade, just behind his stepson. Both men were unwilling subjects for her practice shoot. She needed to perfect her manual mode—adjusting ISO and shutter speed settings—to get the ideal couples photograph.

"I don't understand why the camera doesn't know what to focus on. If I center it, why is the second row blurry?"

She was learning to shoot in manual mode. Auto was so much easier.

"Here," he said as he walked toward her with his hands reaching for the camera. Her son stood still as if someone had pushed the pause button on a video. Daylight was burning. The shade was disappearing.

"No," she said and threw her hand up like a stop sign. "I don't want you to touch anything. Just tell me what to do. Don't you understand this is how I learn?"

Her husband stepped back into his position for the pose.

"Okay. Look through the viewfinder. Focus on one of us. See the meter at the bottom of the screen?"

"Yes."

"You want it to register in the middle. That's perfection."

A half-grin snuck onto her son's face, but no one noticed. He was just a warm body.

"I'm one up."

"Okay, then change your ISO," her husband said gently.

When she looked through the lens, she wanted to capture the smallest details. He always went for the big picture. And so together they made a good team. Of course, he took the obligatory three shots—wide, closer, closest. She started with that one thing. Something would speak to her through the viewfinder. A flower, a curve, a ray of light. She was mesmerized by that one thing. Like a child chasing a butterfly, she couldn't see anything else. He rarely saw the butterfly. His focus was on the technical, the camera settings, the aperture, etc. If the meter hit the center, then he felt he had the perfect photo...never mind the composition. If an aberration was in the photo, it was just accepted. She rejected aberrations. They were mistakes in her eyes, not artistic. Her goal was to catch a person in the reflection of someone's eyeball—detail. They bought the Macro lens just for her bent on photography. He was most comfortable using the "Kit" lens, the 24-105mm. It was the perfect match to the full-frame camera he had insisted on, which allowed the photographer to capture more of the picture as opposed to the "crop sensor" camera they previously had, automatically cropping out the edge of the picture, like the crust off a sandwich. He liked the crust on his sandwich, so they got the full-frame camera. The cropping could be left to post-production. That was agreeable to her, because she loved making the magic happen with her image-editing software.

"Leave me enough room to edit," she reminded him frequently. She trusted her own instincts in shooting close-up, but preferred to edit his into close-ups when the photos spoke to her. The whole process was romantic to her. Every photo telling a story, whether it be a paragraph, a chapter, or the whole book. The beginning, the end, or the middle. It spoke to her and she listened for it. Crop me. Use the Rule of Thirds this time. Make me black and white. On that rare occasion, Don't touch me! And she wouldn't. Those were the shots that brought an audible sigh or laugh out of her. Those were the shots that brought her hand to her mouth—the "money shots", as they both liked to call them.

When they reviewed the edited photos together, those were the final images when he would say, "Wow!" Those were the shots they hoped for, searched for. Those were the moments people paid good money for.

In their relationship, he was the camera and she was the lens. She could show him things in this world he might never see without her, and he was the structure—the home base—she needed to be able to capture her talent, to preserve the moments that would leave a testament to her existence.

She had to cut their photography practice short.

"I need a break. We'll come back to it later, when it's not so hot outside."

Once she got back to the house, she started rummaging through desk drawers and closet shelves. She wasn't really looking for anything. She called it organizing. A worn cardboard box splattered with flowers fell from atop another box she had grabbed off a top shelf in the closet. She took the lid off. Inside were treasures from a past life. She thought she had lost them (or discarded them on purpose). But here they were.

Frozen.

Waiting.

Until she was ready. Was she ready? Why now? She had too much to do today to take a trip down memory lane. But once her fingers were holding the smooth, glossy 4x6 windows, she couldn't look away. Looking at them wouldn't change anything. It wouldn't change how she felt, or what had happened. The door was opened now, and all those emotions were invited in for a visit. How long they stayed was up to her. She maintained that much control. She could refocus her attention at any moment. All she had to do was bring the mechanics of her day back to the foreground. This was her way of controlling the outcome, even though the photos in her hand told the story.

She glanced at the clock, 2 o'clock, and decided to give herself thirty minutes to experience again what she once loved. She dug to the bottom of the box. One day I'm going to organize these…if I decide to keep them. The photos were not dated or marked on the back, but she knew plenty of places to track information to assign those details. She pulled a stack from underneath and let the ones on top fall in its place. She didn't have time to fret over the chaos. She held the batch in her left hand and flipped through them with the thumb on her right hand.

The clock was ticking louder.

She stopped when she saw the photo.

Her face softened into a sad smile. She soaked in the perimeter of the photo first. This was safe. Blue sky with streaks of soft white. The remnants of ancient smoke signals? That straight, thin line that told the sky where to stop. Little dots on the distant water representing some essential obligation, but not to this photo. The waves were caught in motion—forever saying cheese.

Her heart stopped, she shivered as a chill covered her body.

There he was. She let her heart open and love him like she did when the photo had forced time, and the ocean, to stand still. Her eyes traced his soft, brown curls wrapped around a fading fedora, his spotty beard, those lips. He saw her looking.

His eyes said, "Join me, the water's not that cold."

But she was afraid. Always had been of things she couldn't control. The ocean, his yearning to throw caution to the wind in every endeavor he undertook. Right now she wanted to run to him, and let him catch her when the sand disappeared from under her feet with the next wave.

His smile said, "I'll catch you."

She knew he would.

And she was back. 2:30. The water receded, erasing any trace back to the deep where it would be stored until she opened the box again. The lid fit taut on the box. Once closed, the roaring in her ears stopped.

As she pushed the box to the back of the top shelf, her husband's voice replayed in her head from their practice that morning.

"You have to know when to break the rules," he said. "If you don't, in a situation like this, you won't be able to see what's right in front of you. So you keep adjusting until the picture shows all the details you want it to show."

Our Last Days
By Vickie McEntire

We were in our rented chairs on the beach. It was early June, so the air temperature was perfect, the water a little cool. I was under the umbrella—my post all week. My husband was in the sun. Sweating. The ocean was consistent. Around 4 o'clock every day, it started creeping toward our chairs. So did the lifeguard who rented them to us.

"It doesn't feel like our last day," I said to my husband.

"You know, I was just thinking the same thing," he said.

"That's strange. I don't ever remember being so at peace on the last day of vacation. I wonder what that means?"

"Maybe we finally learned how to enjoy it."

"Maybe," I said.

I continued the conversation with myself in my own mind, so he could enjoy his last day in peace and quiet. I liked the way I was feeling—not stressed out about cramming more fun into the hours we had left. Just watching the ocean. I realized my blood pressure had probably synced up with the cadence of the waves. Calm and constant. I closed my eyes to listen. Should I grab my cell phone and record it? No, just listen. So I did. We stopped at the pool on the way back to the room and we both enjoyed a frozen Pina Colada. Refreshing. I read two more chapters. He laid with his back toward the sun. Still no feelings of urgency. We finally made it upstairs, got dressed, and went out to eat. Our last meal was delicious. Crab legs, filet mignon, scallops…we took sunset pictures at the pier. Beautiful. It was a Thursday. My youngest son graduated high school a week before. He'll be working all summer, attending orientation, and before we know it, moving into his dorm room. It might be our last vacation together. It might not be. Either way, we enjoyed it.

It was a basically a storage area, but the owners were more than happy to put a couple of tables together for us. There was a refrigerator in one corner with to-go plates piled on top of it. You entered the room through swinging doors, but it was a private space. We held monthly meetings in that back room. We ate grilled fish with hushpuppies, hamburgers and fries, and the occasional birthday cake. We encouraged each other. One of us cried on the way home after the first meeting. Then she figured out how to take the criticism. Constructively.

It was a getting-to-know you, period. It was a time of show-and-tell. Every single one of us brought something different to the table. There was a preacher who had published a book with one of the ten commandments stating the opposite. Thou shalt cheat on thy wife. His wife didn't catch the error either before it went to print. There was the dark horse who wrote about vampires, murder, and mayhem. We had a poet who didn't know it, and a dramatist who flew into the room like she started her stories—right in the middle of a conversation. There was the family historian, who had traced her ancestors back to the caves. There was the humorist, who saw the funny side of everything with wit and sarcasm. There was me—the fly on the wall—probably more pest than promoter, and last, but not least, was the full-time writer who had her pen in everything from a weekly newspaper column to magazine articles to being the editor of a local magazine. As much as we may have complained about the heat (it felt like we were sitting behind the kitchen some days), or the tea or the food, we never complained about having to attend our meetings. We were like moths to a fire. We were writers, and this was our critique group. It was decided our fire, I mean group, had grown too big. So, we split into two groups one night. Spur of the moment. Just like that. Ironic really.

The last time we all sat together in that room, we didn't know it would be our last time to sit together in that room.

I put seven cards on the black conveyer belt. That's all they had that were appropriate for this occasion. I had told myself that I would give her a card every day for the rest of her life. However long that might be. I would go to another dollar store later to get more.

I wanted to capture every good thing she had ever taught me and remind her of each one. I would say it in the cards. Like writing a long letter, only one paragraph at a time. That's all I could handle, but she needed to hear it, and I wanted to say it. So I decided to read the cards to her.

She was in ICU waiting for her cards. I walked in like a nurse, not a daughter. All peppy and smiling, asking her how she was feeling.

"I brought you something," I teased with my eyes.

Her eyes lit up. She turned her head toward me. I read the card. Tears moistened her pillow. I hugged her and wiped her face. I read a new card to her six days in a row. Each time writing about something she had taught me. Always coming around to how much we all loved her.

On the seventh day, my sister was in the room. I explained to her my card system. Like it was a thing. She smiled at me anyway. I remembered I needed to get more cards. I started reading, but couldn't finish. That hospital air really dries your throat out. My sister took the card and finished reading it for me.

"….I cannot imagine a life without you. Your sacrifices to raise six good people have not been in vain. We all should have given you more of us. No matter how long you live, I can never tell you how much I love you. There are not enough words or cards to write them in. I understand you are hanging on for us. We will be okay. I promise. You can go now."

I never bought another card.

The Red, White, and Blue
By Vickie McEntire

"Grandpa, why are barns red?"

"Well, I reckon it's to keep the cows from getting confused and going to sleep in the wrong house."

"Is that true?"

"We could paint our house red and find out," Grandpa bellowed. The little girl giggled.

Grandma smiled. She held a casserole covered with a white dish towel in her lap. The three of them fit just right in the old, blue pickup truck. The heat of summer had forced the windows down.

Amy was six. As usual, her brain was in fine form on this special day. Thinking about the red barns naturally reminded her of something she had done every day in her first year of school.

"I pledge allegiance to the Flag of the United States of America and to the Republic for which it stands, one Nation under God, indivisible, with liberty and justice for all," she recited to her grandparents. Both of them smiled and glanced at each other.

"You know you're supposed to put your right hand over your heart when you say the Pledge of Allegiance," Grandma said.

"And the boys take off their ball caps," Grandpa added.

"We stand up at our desks and face the Flag," Amy said excitedly. "Do you know why there are thirteen red and white stripes?" Before either one of them could answer, she told them. "My teacher said it's for the thirteen colonies that started our country."

Grandma patted Amy on the leg, "That's right, dear." Amy quietly repeated the Pledge several more times to herself.

They drove past a field of blue linseed dancing in the mid-morning light. Grandpa didn't see it. He smiled at a memory from long ago. It took place on the red hills of Georgia. Bright stars had filled the dark blue night. He had kissed her the first time on the 4th of July. In his mind, all the fireworks since then were a celebration of the best choice he had made in his life.

Grandma remembered her daddy, a WWII veteran, explaining proper flag etiquette to her as a young girl. "No part of it should ever touch the ground or any other object," he had told her. He made sure it didn't touch her mother's prized red roses or the white porch rails. He was so handsome in his dress blues.

"Here we are," Grandpa shut off the engine. A line of vehicles was already parked in front of the big red barn. Tables covered in white collected the food. The sky was a perfect blue.

Two Tales to Make You Laugh
By: Elizabeth Amonett

Our loved one was finally on the road to recovery and worry melted from my countenance. After two long days in the hospital, I needed a break. I convinced my baby sister the patient needed sleep and it was time for us to leave for a while. We could explore Lubbock, Texas, grab a nice dinner, and sleep in our hotel room.

This was our first visit to the area and already my expectations had been shattered. When our plane had descended near the skyline, the view of the seven-story high rise was a shock. My depiction of the megacity disintegrated. The time had finally come to satisfy my curiosity of this "big city".

Our eyes were blinded as we escaped our bedside responsibilities to get outdoors, but the beautiful August mid-summer sun hugged my skin and soothed my emotions. My lungs opened up as I anticipated a change in scenery. We had finally set out to explore the sights of Lubbock, Texas, and there was one specific destination on my itinerary. Before long, I found it. We were on the magnificent and regal campus of Texas Tech University.

Well, it's time for full disclosure, I am a huge Auburn University football fan, and I am also a huge fan of our former coach, Tommy Tuberville. Coach Tuberville was the current coach for the TTU Red Raiders, and my excitement grew as we toured the alluring campus he now called home.

I steered the car slowly around the charming campus and after several minutes, I drove out of a curve and the Red Raiders football stadium appeared like a vision. A few football giants dressed in long shorts, dirty jerseys, and white helmets ran around on a small patch of grass. I started to sweat. What's going on, I wondered. Football camp? Practice? Was it possible Coach Tommy Tuberville was nearby? My heart raced like it did when I was a child standing in line to see Santa Claus.

School was not yet in session and the wide-open sun blasted its scorching heat waves down on the campus, so it was basically a ghost town. All of a sudden, I knew it was plausible that Coach Tommy Tuberville could be on campus. If so, there was a chance I could see him and possibly meet him. I was thrilled. By the time reality popped through my dream, I was driving by the athletic offices. I rapidly shared my fantasy with my baby sister. She was happy for a new surrounding and was along for the ride.

I stopped the rental car on the drive in front of the building. It appeared abandoned. The adjacent parking lot was empty. I leaned out the window and snapped pictures of the words, "Athletic Department", each letter deeply etched into the light colored bricks. I had used my newly purchased fancy-do phone because it also served as a camera. I'm now very tech-y, you see.

So anyway, the barren facility did not deter me. Coach Tuberville's wife could have dropped him off or his vehicle could have been parked closer to the stadium. It was possible my beloved coach could still be inside.

Since football season was just around the corner, I was already wearing my orange and navy. Of course, I wasn't dressed for game day, but my Auburn t-shirt was advertisement enough. Just in case Tommy was inside and peering out his office window, I stepped out of the car and snapped a few more pictures with my fancy-do phone. No one seemed to notice me.

I was not deterred, but I will confess a little disappointed. But this was only the first stop on my expedition. I turned the car around and drove back to the stadium where I had already seen a buzz of activity.

I rolled into the parking lot near the stadium and parked. The gates were wide open. The seats were empty of enthusiastic fans, but wow, it was still an awesome and breathtaking view. I easily and clearly imagined thousands of cheering fans on game day.

However, in hindsight, I had been completely unaware of how exhausted and hungry my sister was. Apparently, her thoughts had drifted to food and getting back to the hotel for some rest and relaxation. But, the only words I ever heard her say over and over again was, "Tommy *who*?"

"He is such an awesome coach, and if it were up to me, Tommy Tuberville would still be Auburn's head coach," I had explained to my baby sister with strong conviction as I wrapped up my ramblings on Auburn college football and Coach Tommy Tuberville.

And yet, after all the detailed opinions and facts regarding these very important matters, the response from my sister was, "Tommy who?"

"Never mind," I said. "Do you want to walk to the stadium with me?"

"No, I can see it from here. I'll just sit here and wait."

"Okay. I'll be right back."

It was obvious I had *some* compassion for my baby sister. It ended up being as hot as Hades and as humid as a sauna, so I had kindly left the car engine running and the air-conditioner furiously blowing *just* for her. I got out of the car.

Like a hunter stalking his prey, I strolled up to the edge of the massive concrete surrounding the entrance into the stadium. I didn't want to sweat anymore and I decided on a careful plan to act casually. I inched forward. The view of the stadium became even more picturesque. I snapped my phone a few times.

I needed, okay... I wanted... to get closer. I crept onward. I had one eye on the stadium and the other eye on three men near the gate. They still were unaware of my presence. I concluded they were gardeners. They were loading lawn equipment into the back of a plain white box-truck.

I was spotted. I stopped dead in my tracks. He spoke a foreign tongue and the other two men turned their gaze in my direction. Their movements slowed. It reminded me of how I will sometimes pause an action movie for a bathroom break, motion within a still picture.

Worker one was hunched inside the back of the truck. Worker two was holding a leaf blower and lifting it up to worker one. Worker three, the short man who saw me, was bent at the waist hoisting a chainsaw up from the ground. Our eyes had locked. Our wide-eyed stares froze time.

I smiled my sweetest smile, picked up my pace and spoke quickly. "I'm just going to get a few pictures of the stadium," I said. I bravely pointed to my new fancy-do phone and continued to walk past them. They were unfazed. I slowed my pace and smiled again. I held up my fancy-do phone and pointed at it. I spoke slowly. "Seeee? I just...want...to take...a...picture of the sta...di...um..." I pointed to the stadium.

Nothing. Man number one still squatted in the back of the truck. Man number two was lifting a leaf blower, and man number three was still bent over holding a chainsaw.

I placed my right hand on my right hip and shifted. With nothing to lose, I let the words pour from my mouth. "You see, I'm an Auburn college football fan and our former coach, Tommy Tuberville…"

It was as if the pause button had been released. Movement began. Faces came to life. Heads bobbed up and down. All three conversed in a language I did not understand. I wasn't sure what they thought, but I forged ahead. I almost ran. I stopped at the gates and held up my phone-camera. The sun glared on the small screen. I tried a different angle. It was useless. I placed my phone-camera in what seemed like the correct spot and snapped, snapped, snapped. The clicking sounded like a professional photographer.

If I hadn't been a scaredy cat, I would have trotted on into the stadium, but between the heat and my guilt, I told myself I would respect these three workers. I did not want to get them in trouble, so I turned around and headed back to the car. The men were back to work and had barely noticed me as I approached them, but still, from pure glee, I waved and smiled one last time.

With my back to them, I giggled aloud. I was delighted with myself and reveled in my accomplishments. I had acted bravely. I had gotten past the guards, well, three gardeners, but they might as well have been guards, and although I had not seen the coach, I had seen the glorious Red Raiders home field up close and empty.

I decided to text these fabulous photos to my sweetheart back home with messages that implied I had met the coach and was given a personal tour. My thoughts constructed the words I would use, and I laughed again at my plot and I marveled over my plan. I was such a sly and clever … "Uhh...where did I park the car?" I literally said out loud.

There was a building in front of me. I stopped, turned back, and looked around. I was at the end of the mostly filled parking lot. I had a moment of slight panic.

I don't recall this many cars being here. I know I was parked closer to the stadium. Hmm… I scanned the rows of cars. I think the rental car is black. Was it a two-door or four-door? Did it have Texas tags? Was it small or a mid-size? I saw a sign, "Staff Only", I read. Oh, I heard, in my memory, the car rental agent telling me mid-size. Hmm...I wonder if one of these vehicles belong to Coach Tommy Tuberville? This was the staff parking lot and it was near the stadium, after all.

My stomach growled.

I decided to call my baby sister. I grabbed my phone but the blasted sun was merciless. I could not see the screen to dial. I held it up and turned myself in all directions to run from the sun's mean and unrelentless glares. It was no use. I was dripping in sweat. I shoved the phone in my back pocket and deliberately trudged through the car lot back toward the stadium examining each row of cars and searching for a two-door or a four-door black car.

I heard the hum of an engine. "Oh yes," I said out loud. "I left the car running."

I trotted toward the sound of the running engine…

I stopped abruptly. "Nope. I had left my sister sitting in the passenger seat. In this red car sat an older woman in the driver's seat. "Argh…" I wiped sweat from my face. At least I had a clue. Look and listen for a mid-sized black car with its engine humming. I continued my methodical search. Before I knew it, I was back at the stadium. I waved to the workers and turned back around.

Did my baby sister move the car on me for payback of the same prank I had pulled on her and my other sisters last Christmas?

My sister from Texas had come home for Christmas and was using my car. My sweetheart and I pulled up into the grocery store parking lot and saw my car. I moved it. I got back in my sweetheart's car and we watched from a hidden spot. It was hilarious to watch my sisters and their children search for the car.

I spotted a bench nestled under a tree. It wasn't the same as air conditioning, but it was shaded and I could sit down. *If my baby sister has moved the car, I'll show her. I'm going to wait her out. I'll sit right there on that bench and wait for her to get my attention.*

I headed toward the bench and was about to step off the hot cement of the parking lot and into some thick green grass when I glanced over my shoulder for one last look. Halleluia and what a relief! I saw my baby sister in the passenger seat of an engine running, two-door black car glaring at me.

I shrugged my shoulders with exaggerated emphasis to let her know: What the heck? You just sat there and watched me wander around lost all over this parking lot on this hot, humid day? You don't beep the horn? You can't just roll down the window and yell, "Hey, over here"?

Isn't it amazing what can be said with one shrug?

Her response to me? She shrugged with even more exaggeration. As if to mimic me. Her face looked angry. I was confused. What is wrong with her? What is she trying to say?

I marched to the car, jerked the door open, bent over, and peered in. "Why didn't you help me? Couldn't you see I was lost?" I know I sounded whiney, but it was how I felt. I felt the cool air and wiped my face. Again.

Like hot butter, the angry mask over the angelic features of my baby sister's face softened into child-like giddiness accompanied by an outburst of uncontrollable laughter. Between sobs of laughter and fits of hysteria, she told me what *she* saw.

"I wondered what in the world you were doing," she said. "I saw you walk over and talk to those workers, then I saw you take a picture of the stadium, and then you headed back this way, and just before you got to the car, you turned and walked over that way," she pointed straight ahead.

"So I watched you walk that way and wondered 'Where are you going now?' Then I saw you walk to the end of the parking lot, lift your phone to take more pictures, and I had to unbuckle my seatbelt to stretch my neck far enough to see what in heaven's name you were taking a picture of. I couldn't see anything picture worthy. I even considered getting out of the car to walk your way and see for myself."

By this time, we sound like a couple of hyenas. She continued.

"Finally, you put the phone away and begin walking back towards our car, but just when I think you're going to get in and drive us to a restaurant, you walk that way, over there toward that bench. I got so frustrated and thought, 'Are we ever going to leave? I'm ready to eat and go back to the hotel. What is she planning now? Is she going to sit down under that tree and just leave me sitting here?' Then finally you turn my way and shrugged a 'what-are-you-doing and why don't you come sit with me on the bench?' shrug. I blew a gasket. I thought 'Me? What are you doing? I'm the one sitting here hot, starving, tired, and patiently waiting on you while you wander around an empty parking lot searching for Tommy somebody.'"

We rubbed away tears of laughter as I explained my side of the story.

When I finished informing my baby sister about the truth of my outing, I grabbed my phone to view and share with her the pictures I had taken…

"What?"

I wasn't laughing anymore.

"Oh no," I said. "Something is wrong with my phone-camera. The only image in my gallery was a picture of my finger covering up most of the frame. There was another image revealing a large white arrow. It proved to be a start button for a video. I hit the arrow and a moving picture of my sandaled feet with freshly painted orange toenails were getting out of the car. The black car door and grey interior, by the way, was clearly visible. The sound was muffled, except the distinct slam of the car door. My baby sister and I looked at each other and after a moment of recognition of what we had just seen, we exploded again with laughter.

***

I would like to share one more story, and I'll give you the quick, abbreviated version.

A young man I know sped 70 mph down a country road. The speed limit was 45. He was driving North when a southbound patrol car passed him. A single blue light flashed before the officer drove around a curve.

My sweet-natured friend had proudly received his driver's license just a few months prior. He had worked all day, had showered, and was on his way to pick up his girlfriend for their Saturday night date. She lived with her grandfather who also happened to be my friend's pastor. He was close to his destination. He looked in the rearview mirror. Nothing. He sped up. His turn was just a few feet away. Once again, he snuck a peek into the rearview mirror as he turned left onto the dirt road leading to his pastor's home. Oops. He hit the stop sign that was strategically placed for those on the dirt road preparing to turn onto the paved road.

"Oh man" he said. "At least there's no cop." He removed his foot from the gas pedal and slowly turned right into the pastor's gravel driveway. He sighed and thought, "If I had come home with a ticket, Dad would have killed me."

"Get out of the vehicle with your hands up!"

"What …" My friend moved the gearshift to park. Flashing blue lights blinded him on this dusky evening right before dark.

"I said get out of the vehicle with your hands up!"

As a deer in headlights and leaving the truck running, my friend stepped out of it with the wobbly knees of a newborn colt. His hands were lifted high like he so often did when he praised the Lord in church. He saw only a gun. He thought he might throw up.

"Turn around! Put your hands on the vehicle and spread your legs!"

My scared young friend did as he was told. The officer ran up to him, frisked him, and removed his wallet from his shaking jeans.

"Can I call my dad?" My friend asked. He willed himself not to vomit and forced himself not to cry.

Another officer drove up. "Help me Lord," my friend cried.

My friend was hauled off to jail and there is a picture of his fingerprints on file. When he was allowed his one call, he called his dad. His truck had been towed away. His parents made him pay the fee. He also was made to pay the charges for speeding. He had to repair the stop sign. The "running from a police officer" charges were graciously dropped. When the kid was released from his cell, he walked skittishly, but freely into the front room of the station and saw his crying mother. His father was livid. His pastor was laughing.

His response to me? "Oh, I drive the speed limit for sure. I understand my mistake and how the officer thought I was fleeing, and I'm not making excuses, I'm just saying there is a difference between running from the law and hiding from the law."

Lover's Leap
By Paul Moses

Two distraught young Cherokee lovers, Takatoka and Falling Blossom, frustrated with their families' refusal to let them wed, held hands and stepped off a high, rocky precipice, thus adding to the preponderance of evidence that in all times of history and in all cultures teenagers do stupid things. In response, the local Council Fire declared that the cliff should receive a special name, not necessarily in honor of the ill-fated couple, but as a warning to other adolescents that following their example was a bad idea (One Council Fire member proposed that they simply build a fence, but he was fired from the government for suggesting something so practical and unromantic).

The Council Fire presented a list of names and everyone voted. The winner was "Lover's Leap". Many considered this a safe choice, given the political importance of the families involved and the widespread unpopularity of the incredibly annoying teenage couple. The close runner up, by the way, was the name "Good Riddance".

On the day after Takatoka and Falling Blossom took their fateful plunge, the Council Fire sent a band of Cherokee braves to the bottom of the cliff to retrieve the broken bodies. The braves, however, found nothing. No bodies. Not so much as a hair or a tooth. Nothing. Nor was there any evidence that the bodies had been spirited away by people or dragged away by hungry animals. A large search party was organized and fanned out all over that side of the mountain. But, alas, nothing.

In time, the legend of Lover's Leap settled into the comfortable grooves of Cherokee folklore and glided smoothly down through the generations, mutating and growing into a bigger lie as it went.

As for Lover's Leap itself, it continued to claim new victims. A Spanish Conquistador, Juan Jose Felipe Maximiliano, attempted to plant his queen's flag on the cliff's stony edge, sneezed, slipped and was never seen again. Something about the Holy Mother was heard as his pointy-toed boots disappeared over the side. As before, nobody was ever found. Not so much as a gauntlet or a mustache comb.

The French explorer Blaise-Augustine Babineaux came to Lover's Leap to explore both the Cherokee legend and as many Cherokee princesses as possible. While enjoying a spectacular sunset and his second bottle of Bordeaux, Blaise-Augustine made an ungainly pass at a certain long-eyelashed Spring Flower and over he went. Yes, gone without a trace. Au revoir, Monsieur Babineaux.

One-Eyed Jack Mablethorpe, the legendary backwoodsman and fur-trader, camped at Lover's Leap, despite his well-documented proclivity for sleepwalking. Enough said.

Sadly, there were others. Mrs. Molly Baker, pioneer woman and one-time whorehouse madam. Captain Abram Woodstock of the Confederate Army. Vaudeville great, Sammy "Sawbones" Swanson, singer, juggler and contortionist. Billy Bunker, free-loving hippie and midnight hiker. Marvin Defoe, cable guy. Gone, all gone. Never found.

As the years passed and the fur trappers gave way to the tourist trappers, Lover's Leap eventually became part of a marketing atrocity known as Rock City. Perched high above scenic Chattanooga, Tennessee, Lover's Leap attracted more and more victims to its perilous edge. Fat camera-toting, flip-flop-wearing salesmen from Omaha and giddy, mildly inebriated college students from parts unknown all flocked to the cliff's edge to snap selfies and test their bravado. The unaccompanied children of inattentive parents swarmed the mountaintop lookout, dancing precariously close to oblivion. Every once in a while a foot would slip and—poof—well, you know.

A tiny planet circles the star at one extremity of Ursa Major, the constellation known as the Great Bear. The planet is Tica-toto-natoo and the star is Alkaid (at the very tip of the handle of the Big Dipper).

On the north-east coast of the largest continent of Tica-toto-natoo, is the capital city Nini-popo-lootoo. At the very center of Nini-popo-lootoo is a small, shallow lake known for countless centuries as The Pool of the Monarchs. This body of water is the most sacred of places for the reptilian-like peoples of Tica-toto-natoo because it is here that the sky god Jebba-niti-jootoo periodically provides his people with a new ruler for their planet.

Around the perimeter of The Pool of the Monarchs stands, like grim sentries, a ring of statues carved with breathtaking skill and beauty from glistening jade-like stone. These startling works of art are memorials to the great monarchs of the past that Jebba-niti-jootoo, in his most superlative and infinite wisdom, provided to his beloved lizard people.

There are statues of the co-regents, Takatoka and Falling Blossom, holding hands.

There is a carving of Babineaux, the drinking king, leaning on a vat of wine.

King One-eyed Jack with his eye closed.

Her Highness Molly Baker, the Virgin Queen.

King Sammy "Sawbones" Swanson, holding his left foot behind his right ear.

His Excellency Billy Bunker, with some sort of ceremonial weed smoking from his lips.

And Marvin Defoe, known as the Comcast King.

These monarchs, and many more, are highly revered and receive constant homage from the Tica-toto-natootians. Incense rises day and night from the finely carved feet of these much-adored emperors.

The reptilian folk live in a constant state of excitement and anticipation, for they never know when Jebba-niti-jootoo will bless them with a brand-new ruler. It could happen at any time of day or night. When it does, a bright light flashes from mid-air about fifteen feet above the center of The Pool of the Monarchs, and—kerplunk!—the new king or queen drops into the sacred waters. Praise be to Jebba-niti-jootoo!

When this happens, the capital city is shocked into an immediate state of jubilant celebration. The new monarch is fished out of the water, dried off, and crowned as Ruler of the Planet. The previous monarch, with great pomp and ceremony, is killed and eaten by all present in a coronation feast known as "Thanksgiving".

Missing Marv
By Paul Moses

Sitting up on the side of the bed, Ramona slipped her feet into the worn flatness of her house shoes and reached for her robe. She sat there for a minute, contemplating sliding back under the toasty covers and watching Good Morning America. She just loved her some George Stephanopoulos. Deciding against this indulgence, she creaked to her feet. She skipped her eyes across the photograph of her late husband, made a little humphing sound, and said, "Well, Marv's been dead now for exactly three weeks. I wonder if he's found anything wrong with Jesus yet."

Ramona thought Marv had a lot of nerve dropping dead right between Thanksgiving and Christmas. The very idea! But—that was just like Marv. Whatever it took to be disagreeable and weasel out of a few chores. He always complained about his "poor ole aching back" when it was time to schlep all the decorations down from the attic. Looked for any excuse to not do it. Well, he finally got his reason.

And a heart attack? Really? Was that completely necessary? Never had anyone in his whole family lineage ever done such a thing. All the way back to Ellis Island, or the Mayflower or whatever, they all had the decency to give a body some notice. Even Marv's two older brothers had died slow, agonizing deaths like anyone with good manners would. At least their wives had a chance to tidy the place up a bit before mourners descended on them like the ten plagues of Egypt. As it was, Ramona's house was crawling with people, opening cabinets, rifling through drawers and flushing toilets before Marv's body dropped to room temperature. A little heads-up would have been nice.

But, no, not Marv! He had to die at Provino's in front of God and everybody, with that poor little waitress standing over him with her mouth open. He plopped his head smack-dab in his plate of chicken parmesan, with absolutely zero consideration for how difficult it is to get marinara sauce out of a cheap toupee. That was both hasty and rude. Ramona was sure that Mrs. Stephanopoulos would never have to face such an ordeal. George was sure to contract something that would kill him in a dramatically prolonged manner. He was Greek, after all. Those people have class and know how to leave this world properly.

Ramona shuffled into the kitchen and set the table for breakfast. Two plates, again. She put one back and dropped the bread into the toaster. Two slices, again. She put one back. She heard the newspaper thwack on the front porch, but ignored it. The paper was his thing, not hers. Anything really important in the world would show up on Good Morning America. She made a mental note—another mental note—to cancel the paper subscription. What did the Calhoun Times know anyway? If she really needed to know about it, George would tell her.

As she sipped coffee and crunched marmalade toast, Ramona eyed the ceiling and dreaded her trip to the attic. But the trip must be made, she knew, and Marv wasn't there to do it. Thanks for nothing. The grandkids would be along Christmas Eve, expecting a festively decorated house, so it couldn't be helped. She felt neither joyful nor triumphant.

After changing into her blue jeans, sneakers and favorite tee-shirt (Rolling Stones, 1976 World Tour), she pulled the rope that opened the drop-door to the attic. The fat springs on the door protested with loud, metallic disharmonies. Ramona thought she sympathized. She tiptoed up the moaning wooden ladder-steps and gave the long string a tug. The glaring white bulb swung back and forth, a pendulum chasing shadows.

Where to start? She moved about gingerly, her head tilted to one side to avoid bumping the rafters. Where did he put the Christmas stuff? Here? No, that's Halloween. Is that it? Wrong again. Old scrapbooking. Snow skies? Who snow skies? Yard sale. Golf clubs. Yeah, that infatuation lasted a whole three months. She could have put a down payment on a new car for what those clubs cost. Yard sale. Boxes of old clothes. His mother's hats and gloves. Why did he insist on keeping those old things? Goodwill. Lots of lamp shades, no lamps. Really? Leaf bags full of stuffed animals. To the grandkids? Or maybe the church nursery. A rolled-up carpet. Another rolled-up carpet. And another. Yard sale, yard sale, yard sale. Everything under the sun, except what she was looking for. It was just like Marv to hide the Christmas decorations and then go die right in the middle of the main course. If he were alive she would kill him. Push him down the attic steps, hairpiece over heels.

Something caught her eye. Something red. Ramona navigated through the clutter, ducking under clinking clothes hangers, and came to a stack of boxes with red stickers on them: X-MAS DÉCOR. At last! She reached up to pull the top box down, but found it too heavy for her. Over-packed. Great. Marv never could pack anything. She always told him to spread the heavy stuff around, mixing it with the lighter things. He never listened. Never. And now she would have to unpack all these boxes and rearrange their contents just so she could carry the dang things down the steps. It was just like Marv to over-pack and then skip off through the Pearly Gates before he carried the boxes down. Right after Thanksgiving. Right in the middle of dinner. Right before Christmas. Right when she needed him. "That's just like you, Marvin James McClure!" she shouted, clawing the top box off of the stack and smashing it to the dusty floor.

The box flew open upon impact and belched its contents all around Ramona's feet. She scowled down at the mess, ready, suddenly, to make a once-and-for-all trip to the nearest landfill. But among the spilled tree ornaments she saw a small wrapped package. She knew immediately it was from Marv because it was wrapped in the Sunday funnies. He always wrapped gifts in the Sunday funnies. She hated that. It looked cheap, she thought, but he always insisted that comic strips made people happy. Everybody but her. It was just like Marv to be cheap on the gift wrap and then go toes-up before he could even give the present away.

She moodily kicked the ornaments aside and picked up the gift. There was his handwriting scrawled across Garfield in black Sharpie: "To Ramona From Marv." My, what a way with words, she thought. So original. And heartfelt. He must have sat up all night editing that masterpiece. Ramona felt the edges of the present. Her scowl deepened. A book. She wasn't much of a reader. He knew that. He gave her a book. Just like Marv. A book. She gritted her teeth. He didn't know her. He didn't care. After decades of marriage, two cross-country moves, four kids, nine grandchildren and two mortgages he still didn't have a clue. A BOOK! She reared back to throw the package as hard as she could, but then stopped. All of the energy ran out of her and she lowered her arm to her side. She had to look. She had to know.

Ramona picked her way back to a spot under the bare light bulb. Dismissing one more urge to chuck the gift, she turned it over and peeled the tape off. For some reason, she could not bring herself to tear the Sunday funnies. The paper fell away and she turned the book over. Her breath caught in her throat. The title said: "All Too Human", by George Stephanopoulos. Ramona threatened one side of her mouth with a smile and mumbled, "Oh, Marv, that's just like you. Merry Christmas."

WHERE I CAME FROM

Who we are today is a great indicator of two things. The first is where we came from and the second is what we are capable of. While our past does not define us, it surely has an impact on our lives. Some of us have been provided opportunities that allowed us to flow easily into our callings and have prepared us to make an impact on our world. For others, we have had to fight to overcome great adversity and struggle. Either way, we can look back in life and see pivoting moments that have aligned us with our destiny and then look forward to our future and know just what we are capable of.

There is something to be said about the people of our past. Parents, siblings, friends, neighbors, a favorite teacher….unbeknownst to them, folks are constantly at work shaping the future of others. We invite you to read about some of our stories from way back when. Maybe we can help show you just how much of an impact you can have in the life of someone. And we would love to hear your stories of where you came from as well!

I am Frostproof
By Karli Land

In the small, quaint town of Frostproof, Florida, I am one of many....

I am one of many who spent their young, impressionable years walking the halls of Frostproof Elementary School. One who has listened as the morning announcements crackled their way into the classrooms. One who collected mom and dad's spare change from the dresser in order to visit the F.E.S. School Store to buy a scented marker or a pencil grip. One who dreaded running the mile at P.E. but never stopped running during Field Day at the Bulldog's Stadium. One who stood on the playground and watched for the launch of the Challenger not understanding the magnitude of what happened that day.

I am one of many who spent their summers along the shores of Clinch Lake. One who swam in the weeds along the boat ramp never considering the dangers of an alligator. One who left the water only long enough to sit on the back of a pickup and eat a bologna sandwich. One who waited for a small patch of sand to become available in order to dig with a plastic shovel.

I am one of many who spent barefoot days running down the aisles of Harvey's Convenience Store looking for the candy I needed to calm my craving. One who loved buying a large soda in a Styrofoam cup for 49 cents and always took a peek into the backroom to see if anyone I knew was back there shooting pool.

I am one of many who enjoyed visiting the Frostproof Historical Museum, learning about those who had come and gone, leaving their mark on the precious town. One that loved hearing stories of the Indian burials nearby and of Elvis' visit to the city to visit hometown relatives. One who delighted in seeing the relics of yesteryear housed in the small building with creaking floors and no air-conditioning.

I am one of many who spent countless hours sitting at the feet of a long-haired librarian, listening to tales told with kind eyes and funny voices. One who spent summers knee-deep in glitter and pipe cleaners during the Summer Reading Program and who watched E.T. for the first time hiding tears at the movie's end. One who checked out the maximum number of books allowed out at one time and pushed for mom to read 'just one more' even though the doors were being locked for closing.

I am one of many who waited anxiously as the town with two red lights began clearing land for the coming McDonalds that would make us as big-time as we would ever be. One who applied to work in this happening joint as a first 'real' job and spent many nights and weekends taking orders and shoveling fries. One who dreaded opening day of the McRib season and sat in the parking lot after hours because it was the cool thing to do.

I am one of many who timidly made their way through teenage years at Frostproof High School. One who spent Friday nights on a football field puffing away into the mouthpiece of a clarinet under many layers of a band uniform. One who went through the lunch line hoping that a smile to the lunch lady would win you the biggest cookie. One who dreaded Algebra I although the teacher was really one of the best. One who struggled with the locker combinations and hated taking the stairs between classes. One who sold ribbons in Homeroom as a member of the Pep Club. One who felt a sense of pride with every Frostproof Bulldog football win.

I am one of many who said goodbye to loved ones besides mounds of dirt at the Silver Hill Cemetery. One who still weeps over lives lost and spends nights wishing to go back in time for one last moment. One who walks the rows reading the names so familiar and thinking about life after our walk on this earth is done.

I am one of many who has moved on and found their way to other places. One whose life has carried them far from their nest and now have made their mark somewhere new. One who now lives among people who have never heard of Frostproof, Florida and always want to know how it got its name. One who will continue to tell the tales of the sweet town and its wonderful people trying to represent it well.

To members of my hometown, I am one of many. But to outsiders, I am Frostproof, Florida.

We Are The Amonetts
By Elizabeth Amonett

I have fifty first cousins on daddy's side of the family, but the Kennedys we ain't!

We are the Amonetts.

Daddy was one of thirteen children born to Curtis and Nina Amonett. Curtis and Nina are the patriarch and matriarch of our family, and *everyone* calls them "Poppy" and "Grandma Amonett". Daddy, his siblings, and their parents were a tightknit group who taught us cousins to fear God, value family, and work hard.

Compared to the financial wealth and Harvard educations of the Kennedy family, many in our family live below the poverty line and, too many, are uneducated. Only a few of us were able to attend college.

However, daddy taught me a lesson regarding the measure of wealth. We once had a conversation about President Franklin Roosevelt and the New Deal Act, specifically the Homestead Communities program. I asked him if Poppy and Grandma Amonett had applied for housing in the Tennessee Homestead Community during the depression. (From the 2,000 applicants received in two weeks, only 250 families were accepted.) Daddy's reply?

"Why no, Sis, that was for poor people."

I was shocked. "I thought we were poor people?!"

"Oh, Honey," he said, "back then, people were starving. There was no food, and soup lines were miles long. Now don't get me wrong, Sis, we had hard living, but we always had a piece of land for farming, a creek nearby for fishing, and guns and ammo for hunting. We walked barefoot, but we was rich cuz we had food."

It was a proud moment for me.

As mentioned earlier, most in our enormous family were not college-bound. Daddy, himself, had no formal education of any kind. In the late 1930s, a mule kicked him in his head, and the injury to his eye was critical. The doctor advised his parents to keep him home from school, and they did. Even after daddy healed, he never returned.

Daddy told me, "Sis, I'm the only kid whoever played hookie from home and ran away to school. I'd stand outside the classroom and lean into the open window until the teacher let me in. My brother and sisters kept my secret, and Mommy never knew."

As an adult, daddy was tested and scored at a second-grade reading level. It was at this time he learned to write his name. Afterward, he no longer signed documents with an 'X' mark. I still recall the glimmer of pride in his smile as he demonstrated to me how he had learned to write his name. I was fifteen years old.

Consider this: Daddy loved to travel, and often did, but the next time you take a road trip, imagine how it would be if you could not read any road signs. Daddy managed his handicap fairly well, and concealed his disability whenever possible. He was a proud man who walked, talked, and dressed *his* way. His personality was larger than life. Using his own self-description, he was a genuine east Tennessee mountain man who loved people, and people loved him.

Yes, my daddy was illiterate, but he loved and valued people. This gift along with his common-sense understanding and his unending thirst for knowledge made him one of the wisest people I've ever known. He spoke simple words, yet taught me profound and valuable life lessons. Several of his lessons started with, "Poppy always said."

One of my favorites?:

"Sis, Poppy always said, the President of the United States and the janitor of the White House both put their pants on one leg at a time. You ain't no better than anybody else and ain't nobody else any better than you, but you gotta remember to always be kind and value people above all else."

Within a large family, the variety of personalities multiply, and thereby it increases the overall odds for drama, and we Amonett's have had plenty of drama. Fortunately for us, though, our scandals, tragedies, and devastations never made national headlines like those in the Kennedy family have.

However, in my opinion, outsiders often view and judge entire families by the actions of one. While our family is there for each other, the truth is no matter how large and supportive a family may be, in the end, everyone is accountable for themselves and must walk their own life-path. Each person is and should be seen as an individual. In fact, the Amonetts have more types of characters than Baskin Robbins has ice cream flavors.

There are some Amonetts who appear to have it all—love, prosperity, and good health -- and yet, they seem unhappy. While other Amonetts have survived hellish circumstances and, even if they had experienced moments of hopelessness, they somehow persevered and chose to live victoriously. They are the ones who seem to glow with happiness.

Living between these two extremes are kinfolk who hide behind masks of bitterness, anger, and spite. A few more take pleasure in blaming the world for their misfortunes. Sadly, there are others who limp along with shame and guilt. A handful seldom find peace, and these wounded coexist with those wearing rose-colored glasses refusing to face reality. Some walk aimlessly, others with purpose. The personalities are as wide as the numbers are deep.

Sadly, as many families do, we, too, carry a mantle of dysfunction. But examine closer and you'll see that our broken and damaged are merely just beautifully weathered antiques. In truth, they are the most wonderful and priceless spirits in the bunch, and there are many.

Most Amonetts are good-hearted and good-natured souls who love life and possess enough empathy and compassion to breathe new life into dry bones and dead hearts. They live authentic lives and give generously of their love, mercy, and forgiveness. It's their love that covers our dysfunction, and it's their lifestyle that demonstrates the traditions and practices of our inherited Christian faith.

Daddy often said, "Sis, when you ain't got nuttin', family and faith is everything."

In a family our size, not everyone chooses to accept this Christian faith, but everyone was exposed to it.

As for me, I cannot live life victoriously without the Lord. I cling to Him and His Word. It was in the midst of life's worst circumstances that I learned that everything I could ever need or want is found in Him. It's because of my faith in Jesus Christ that I am a happy and contented person.

Now, I don't know if it was a strong faith in God, poverty and lack of education, or if it was all these things playing out in life's storms, but for whatever reasons, Daddy's family had a bloodline mentality that ran much thicker than water.

When I was young, it was fun. I loved the family dropping in and out continuously. Some even came for extended stays, and everyone knew everyone's else's business. When I left home and began my own family, these habits were sometimes annoying.

As time passed, however, I learned to set boundaries and live by them. Eventually, this mentality became priceless and comforting. I saw my family anew, and I was better able to appreciate them and appreciate where we come from.

As Daddy always said, "Sis, everybody's gonna need help at one time or another, and with a large family, you ain't never alone, and there's always somebody around to help ya out." If I heard him say this once, I heard him say it a million times.

So in summary, within our large family, drama is always happening, but we look out for each other. In addition, we recognize that we are individuals accountable for our own actions with our own story to tell, but we, also, have a shared history.

So now that things are clear as mud, let me explain. The following story is mine, but it belongs to all of us, and it is the very heartbeat of Daddy's family.

Like the Kennedys, we, too, are bound by blood, by name, and by shared heritage. This biography is part of the Amonett heritage.

#

I was born in 1961, and for every year of my life, my daddy's kinfolks have gathered at the family cemetery on Decoration Day— otherwise known as Memorial Day.

Daddy was born on the third day of June 1934 and for every year of *his* life, no matter where his wandering feet were, come the end of May, on Decoration Day he would most certainly be found moseying along familiar paths that wind around our family's graves.

Going to the cemetery at least once a year for all these years, I've had the privilege of hearing many stories about my living and dead family members. Yes, there are legends sprinkled in with truth, but isn't that what folklore is?

I was told that Decoration Day began weeks after the Civil War when former slaves had stumbled upon a mass grave filled with dead soldiers from the Union army. The newly freedmen dug up the deceased veterans and gave them a proper burial and then held a dedication ceremony.

That solemn act of kindness was the seed for a yearly event that is still held to this day. Through the passing of time, the annual tradition intertwined with multiple cultures and practices from all around our nation and at the same time was being gently sifted through an ever changing political climate. The end result is the current holiday known as Memorial Day, the day our country honors the men and women who have died in military service.

However, for Poppy and Grandma Amonett, Decoration Day 1935 became more than a formal remembrance for honoring veterans from the Union and Confederate Civil War. It marked the beginning of a deep, personal, and heartfelt family tradition.

It was February 1935, and my grandparents teenage daughter was staying with their eldest daughter to assist her during her pregnancy. Their oldest son was, also, not at home. Thank God, because on a cold, hellish night, witnesses say Nina ran from the house with her hair in flames, carrying a crying baby, who was my six-month-old daddy. Poppy was right behind her dragging their four-year-old son by his ankles. Nina fell to the ground with her hair burned and smelly, and Poppy— whose skin was described as a copper color and who later developed lifetime scars—crumbled to the dirt beside her. Together, they watched their home burn to the ground. Four of their children were still inside. They didn't make it out.

Poppy and Grandma Amonett buried the remains of their four children next to their infant son who had died two years earlier from pneumonia. Their baby daughter, Evelyn, was buried in a different family cemetery a few miles away. I cannot fathom my grandparent's grief.

I do know; however, whenever the family discussed the past, it was defined as before the fire or after the fire. I also know how dedicated Daddy was to his two baby sisters born after the fire and how dedicated all his siblings were to each other and to their parents. The family was like glue, and stuck together through thick and thin.

And like a mother goose, Grandma Amonett led her goslings to the cemetery every Decoration Day, beginning in May 1935, to place flowers on her children's graves. She continued this annual pilgrimage until 1959. That fateful Memorial Day was her last. She died that very day in an automobile accident while en route to purchase new flowers.

There were eight in the car. Four died—my Grandma Amonett, Nina; *her* mother; her infant granddaughter; and her young nephew. Some of our surviving family still remember seeing the four coffins at the front of the church.

After Grandma Amonett died, Poppy continued their practices. He lead his family on the annual journey to the cemetery. Flowers were placed on the graves of his children, his wife, and all the loved ones lost. After Poppy joined Grandma Amonett in eternity, their surviving children, grandchildren and great-grandchildren picked up the baton and carried on their tradition.

Today, the grassy meadow is adorned with an over-abundance of various-sized tombstones, and their scattered appearance seems to suggest someone once had a straighter plan, but our activities on Decoration Day rarely change. We meet and greet. We walk the narrow, hilly trails between burial plots. We reflect upon treasured memories while reading familiar names engraved on what my daddy called "tomb rocks". Then the endearing hard work begins. Tombstones are cleaned. Weeds are pulled, and the dead, faded flowers are trashed. Sometimes, extra topsoil is brought in to level out shifting ground, and new sod is laid. The sweet and final step to this family ritual is to blanket the graves with colorful, fresh décor.

In the early years, when Grandma Amonett was alive, she picked fresh flowers or crafted paper mache flowers until store-bought flowers became available. Nowadays, bouquets of silk flowers splash a rainbow of vibrant colors all across the evergreen canvas of the Tennessee family cemetery.

"It shore is purty," my daddy would say, "and it shows respect."

There are no rules, and each immediate family has their own ideas, so decorations are inconsistent, and yet, perfect at the same time. There is reassuring structure in our comfortable routine.

When the work is done, the large crowd of extended family huddles into one massive clump for an emotional prayer and a quick word of thanks for the food we are about to devour. The scrumptious potluck meal spreads across three wooden picnic tables. The tables were built long ago and placed under a shelter bordering a small playground area.

The swings and merry-go-round were added after my youth. Someone decided the playground was needed in order to entertain the smaller children. Their light-hearted laughter is the perfect bookend to the soberness, tears, and sadness of the elderly. The young and old family-size bookends are what holds our middle generations together.

After filling our bellies with some of the best tasting home-cooked foods ever to be found in the state of Tennessee, the majority of our group circles around the elders and that's when the talented souls bring out guitars, banjos, and any other instruments brought in for the event. The gifted musicians who, sadly, most of the world has never heard, start tuning up their strings and then they play.

The lovely music pours out over the cemetery and seeps into the valley my daddy called a "holler."

"You know, Sis," he explained to me when I asked him as a child, "a holler, it's the place between two mountains."

A melodic symphony echos in the holler with a beautiful arrangement composed of stringed instruments and family harmonies. Lyrics that range from a mixture of modern day praise and worship tunes to the old, but never worn-out traditional hymns are belted throughout. Everyone has a favorite song.

When I was a little girl, I was mesmerized by the beautiful sound.

My favorite song then was the classic, "Will the Circle Be Unbroken," and as I look back, I smile at the memory of Daddy lowering his head and twisting his chin just right in order to reach down deep into his chest and pull out his handsomely sung bass notes. He also sang bass on another classic song entitled, "Let Us Have a Little Talk With Jesus." It's a favorite, too. I can't pick just one!

The song on my heart these days, though, is the worship melody called, "Lord, I Give You My Heart." It's special because it reminds me of Mother. I sang the song to Mom a gazillion times as she lay drifting away from my sisters and me while under under the care of Hospice. I sang the song into her left ear, over and over again for hours and hours, until she no longer heard me.

But when it's all said and done, the crème de la crème for my listening ears is when I hear the originally penned lyrics and musical scores that my sister and cousins have beautifully crafted. It truly doesn't get any better than that.

This year will be the same. I will drive through the majestic mountains of Tennessee and meet up with relatives who live nearby and with those who traveled from afar. We will visit, reminisce, and decorate our family's graves.

Per Mother's request, her ashes were spread out over a field of flowers. Daddy, though, is now buried in the family cemetery with his very own special tomb rock. He was placed a few rows back from where his parents, Nina and Poppy, rest.

But the Amonett story did not begin with Poppy and Grandma Amonett.

Poppy's ancestry goes back to the seventeenth century to Jacob Amonett who lived in France. This is where we find our Protestant Christian roots. This long legacy of family and faith is a vine that broadens the Amonett tribe and connects Daddy's immediate family to past ancestors and to future descendants.

Poppy's dad, Sherman Amonett, and his grandfather, James Amonett are both buried a few miles east from the cemetery where Daddy is buried. Up winding roads and steep hills are where you will find those family cemeteries.

Poppy's great-grandfather was Ruben.

Ruben arrived from Virginia and settled in the rich, luscious East Tennessee soil in 1810 after the death of his father, William Amonett. He came with a dream to build a home and grow a farm. But he did not live there long. Duty called.

Ruben volunteered to fight with Andrew Jackson in the war of 1812. He died in 1814 at Fort Jackson, Mississippi, from wounds he received in a battle fighting against Creek Indians. He was thirty-nine years old. I do not know where he is buried.

Ruben's father William Amonett was born and raised in Virginia.

William's father, Andrew, was born in Paris, France. Andrew came to Virginia when he was ten years of age. He sailed from England with his father, Jacob Amonett.

Jacob Amonett is my six times great-grandfather. He was born in Loudun, France around 1665. He was a French Huguenot, and in October 1685, King Louis XIV had given Huguenots the choice to give up their Protestant faith or die. Jacob fled.

The story goes that Jacob Amonett was privileged. He came from wealth and influence, and therefore, was able to flee France. He took refuge in The Hague, Holland and served Prince William of Orange who, after the Glorious Revolution, became King of England reigning with his wife Mary as Queen. In 1697, England and its allies signed a peace treaty with France, but the treaty made it impossible for Huguenots to return to their homeland. Jacob left for Virginia in late 1700.

The name William is a popular within the Amonett family. I've heard it said the reason is because of the gratitude Jacob and his family had toward King William. The king extended them, and other Huguenot refugees, kind compassion, financial aid, and hope.

King William was forced to manage the influx of French refugees. One solution he offered was to provide Huguenots with passage to the American Colonies and give them land and religious freedom. Legend is that Jacob Amonett was loyal to King William, and in return, the king knighted him. Then, in 1700, Jacob Amonett set sail from England on the "Nassau" with his wife and four children to Virginia.

My four, five, and six times great-grandfathers, William, Andrew, and Jacob, lived and died near Richmond, Virginia. I tried to find their graves a few years ago, but the family homestead and burial plots are gone. In its place is a mall , so I have no clear knowledge of where my grandfathers are buried.

I was, however, able to visit the community to which Jacob and his family migrated to and lived in for many years-Manakintown, Virginia near the James River. While visiting, I toured the church my Jacob and later Andrew helped to establish. The existing Manakin Episcopal Church is located near the headquarters and library of The Huguenot Society of the Manakin in the Colony of Virginia.

The present day church is the fifth building for the congregation. It was built in 1954.

The fourth structure was constructed in 1895, and almost one hundred years later, the vestrymen donated it to the Huguenot Society. The beautifully crafted church is well loved and currently maintained by the Society. To this day, it is still used for special occasions.

Upon entering the old, historical church, the glossy white pews appear heavenly. It was a perfect summer day when I walked up the middle aisle and saw gold-colored plates attached to the end of each pew. The plates were engraved with the names of the founding members, and on the front row of the left hand side of the sanctuary was the shiniest gold colored name-plate of all. It read, Jacob Amonett.

I wish my Daddy could have made that trip, but I felt his spirit. He and the generations that connect me to Jacob Amonett seem but just a short distance in time.

When I was a child, I enjoyed going with my daddy to the family cemetery on Decoration Day, in part, because I got to play with my cousins. As a young adult, however, I dreaded the expense, the effort, and the clear choice of how my holiday should be spent, but dutifully, I did my best to honor the tradition out of respect for my daddy. Without fail, at the end of each holiday weekend, I walked away with priceless memories. But, somewhere along the path of life—about middle age—the trip became emotional and tender, and I *wanted* to make my journey to the family cemetery on Decoration Day.

Now-a-days, I have replaced my daddy as the family sales rep. I talk up and sell the tradition to younger generations who would rather go to the lake. I explain to them how our ritual began and why it is so important to the legacy of our family.

The graveyard is crowded. The family members who attend have dwindled. But each year on Decoration Day, I travel to Tennessee and visit the family cemetery. I plan to continue this pilgrimage for as long as I am able. I know how much it meant to my daddy-- and to his family, and I can finally admit, after he is no longer here for me to say to him, it means alot to me, too.

In all these years of tradition, including that mournful day on May 26, 2009, days after the official Decoration Day when my sisters and I had to purchase a tomb rock for our daddy, I've heard the most interesting, delightful, and funny stories ever told concerning our long history and enormously extended family. My voracious appetite is never satisfied for more of these types of stories.

Daddy's gone, but my passion still burns. I want to learn more about where I come from and who it is that brought me here.

Along the way, I have learned some Huguenot history. The more I knew, the more I wondered about the plight of Huguenots and specifically about the life of my ancestor, Jacob Amonett. What was it like for him living in France during this horrific time of persecution? What was the path of his journey leaving France in 1685 before finally arriving in Virginia in 1701? What happened after he arrived? As I considered these things, history became alive and personal. As I laid my imaginations over the template of history, a love for Jacob Amonett grew.

But I have also fallen in love with Jacob's son, Andrew, and with Andrew's son William, who lived during the years of the Revolutionary war. Was William a Patriot or Loyalist?

I am in love with William's son, Ruben Amonett, who settled in Tennessee and died leaving his four year old son James. James was Poppy's grandfather.

I'm in love with Sherman who was the son of James and Poppy's dad.

I've always loved Curtis Amonett, who is my Poppy.

These men are not just names on a tombstone. They are my grandfathers.

Poppy fell in love with Nina, my Grandma Amonett. They married and created a loving family of their own, and it's because of them, I have Daddy. I belong to him.

Yes, Daddy's family suffered, but so did Jacob Amonett's family, and so did all the generations in between them, but each man lived his life. Each married, had children, survived tragedy, and had their own story to tell.

I feel a connection to Jacob Amonett. I think he would be proud of our family. His family. He fled France with hope of escaping. He came to the New Colonies with hope of finding a place to call home, and he did.

Jacob Amonett provided his family and their descendants an opportunity to make a life for themselves in a place where they could worship God freely and make their own choices—good or bad—of their own free will, without oppression from any king or from any government. I am Jacob's descendant. I am an Amonett, a committed Christian, and a proud American. And for all these things, I am grateful.

Where I Came From
By Amber Nagle

Before I moved to the foothills of Appalachia, I was a flatlander—a barefooted native to a warmer region accentuated with millions of towering pine trees and void of significant hills. Bonaire is a small town tucked in the geographic center of Georgia—just south of Warner Robins, which is just south of stinky old Macon, which when I was a child, housed a paper mill that emitted a foul stench that smelled like rotten eggs and tainted the freshness of the dawny dew every single morning. To the east, the landscape is bordered by the wide and muddy Ocmulgee River and the sprawling concrete flight lines of Robins Air Force Base. To the west, I-75 cuts through acres and acres of peach trees with their pinkish-purple blossoms that bask in the bright sunshine of spring before fruits as large as softballs emerge in the summertime and weight the branches like boat anchors.

I was born in 1965, a tumultuous year in history wedged between the assassinations of President John F. Kennedy and Martin Luther King, Jr. It was the year that our country began sending thousands of our young men overseas to fight in Vietnam and just a few years before the first man walked on the moon.

I attended brainy Honors classes at Warner Robins High School, where I was also a twirler in the band, president of the Beta Club, a long-distance runner on the track team, and a Thespian. Our powerhouse football team had won two AAAA national championships by the time I was a senior, and almost everyone on the south side of town attended the Friday night games. Our mascot was a demon, and someone in town had built a twenty-foot-tall, red devil sculpture out of paper mache with flashing green eyes and a pitchfork to roll out at the football games. Every time the football team scored a touchdown or field goal, the big demon monster shot fireworks from the tines of his pitchfork, our band would break into a spirited rendition of "Dixie," and spectators would clap along and wave giant rebel flags in the stands. Several local African Americans in the community came forward to say that the fight song and flags were offensive to them. It was a time before computers and the Internet, and so many of us didn't even realize the negative history connected to the fight song or the flag. The controversy continued through my senior year and divided our community along racial lines. Seeing both sides of the argument, I was trapped in the middle.

That's where I came from.

Like other military towns, Warner Robins and Bonaire are rocked frequently by sonic booms and low-flying aircraft. The official motto is EDIMGIAFAD, which is a crazy, long acronym for "Every Day in Middle Georgia Is Armed Forces Appreciation Day." The area is an amalgam of different cultures, races, religions, and ethnicities—a melting pot that for me, nurtured diversity acceptance, understanding, and patriotism. The Air Force Base was, and still is, the lifeblood of the area, and it was the lifeblood of our household.

After my dad's service as a paratrooper in the U.S. Army, he found work as a civilian at the Air Force Base. He supervised workers at an air freight terminal on the flight line and worked a brutal rotating shift—several weeks on day shift, then several weeks on swing shift, then several weeks on night shift. In the decades before September 11th, security was lenient, and I often pulled up to the gate and said, "I need to take a sandwich to my father. He's working swing shift and works on the flight line." The gate guards never questioned my motives—just stepped back and waved me in. I drove the family sedan onto the flight line past C-130s and F-15 fighter jets being serviced and right up to the doorway of my dad's building, then skipped into his building unchallenged to deliver the contents of a brown paper sack to him. He and I walked around for a few minutes through a maze of boxes and conveyors saying "hello" to his coworkers before I jumped back into the car and drove home.

My dad also co-owned a trailer hitch installation shop with my Uncle Edwin in Macon. My mother was the bookkeeper, and so my siblings and I spent a lot of time at the shop. It was a dangerous place for children to play.

"Don't look back there! I mean it!" Mom or Dad would say when someone was welding, but I always peeked and saw something that resembled yellow fireworks shooting from the tip of the welder—as bright as the sun in the August sky. Luckily, I never kept my gaze for long enough for the arc to burn my eyes, but my father was not so fortunate. Working around welders made him a bit careless, and his eyes were burned so severely a few times during my childhood, that my mother had to carry him to the emergency room.

So my dad worked a lot and made it his mission in life to provide for the family and send the three of us to college, and he fulfilled that mission. Aside from being father to three, a husband, and a workaholic, he was also a whistler, a hummer, a mumbler, a gardener, a hunter, a fisherman, a gun and knife collector, a walker of woods, a beekeeper, a drinker of bourbon and Coke, a player of cards, a pool shark, a watcher of Westerns, a diehard sports fan, a fearer of snakes, a wearer of ball caps, a Mason, a collector of coins, arrowheads, and buckeyes, a man who could stay mad about nothing for days, and a guy who liked to laugh—hearty, loud belly laughs—from time to time.

To remember his laughter, my mind often travels back to a Christmas day around 1990. My brother's first wife had given my brother a radio-controlled airplane kit. As my dad and husband watched television, and Mom and I prepared Christmas dinner, my brother sat out in my parents' game room alone and constructed the airplane. Around 4 p.m., he announced he was done and ready to launch the airplane replica and watch it take flight. Several of us—me, my husband, my sister-in-law, my dad, and my mom—drove to a flat, vacant piece of property my brother owned to witness the plane soar through the winter sky. Andy smiled, gripped his plane, thrust it forward, then stepped backward with the controller to guide it. We watched the tiny plane go up, and up, and up, and up… then down, and down, and down in a nose dive. It slammed into the earth with great force, to the shock of us all. In the momentary silence, I heard a low cackle and then a muffled roar and then the unleashing of maniacal laughter coming from my father, who was doubled over—tears squirting from his eyes. For whatever reason, the demonstration and destruction of the airplane had touched his funny bone, and he couldn't contain it, so he just let it go.

And I am my father's daughter—known for laughing at somewhat inappropriate times. I also have his deep-set eyes (though mine are brown), his tall lumbering gait, his mechanical inclinations, his nose, his work ethic, his love of the great outdoors, and sometimes—his darkness.

That's where I came from.

We lived in a large ranch-style house filled with avocado appliances, gold shag carpeting, green vinyl flooring, and the paneled and wallpapered walls prevalent in Seventies decor. My siblings and I ran wild like animals—riding our bikes and skateboards up and down the streets of the neighborhood, building ramps and jumping ditches like Evel Knievel, taking new neighborhood kids on snipe hunts, turning cartwheels across lawns covered with coarse Centipede grass, chasing one another through a field filled with Xanthium plants that affixed velcro-like cockleburs to our shirts and socks as we raced past. Our sheepdog mix, Boaz, ran with us—the spiny cockleburs winding and tangling tightly into his fur until one of us took the time to pull them out.

Our backyard was a playground filled with learning opportunities. High on a tall pole on one side, hollow gourds dangled in the breeze like drop earrings awaiting the arrival of the Purple Martins. We sat in a wooden swing and watched the birds catch insects and feed their ravenous fledglings for hours. Sometimes a baby fell out of a gourd house, and we rushed in and saved it from our cat, who was a great huntress. Then one day, we'd wake to find the Purple Martins gone, like a band of rent jumpers in the night.

On the other side of the yard was a chicken coup filled with egg-laying feathered friends and a crudely constructed basketball goal that my family huddled around regularly to play games of "horse," "around the world," and "21."

In the middle of the yard, my parents had placed a couple of beehives. We watched as my dad—covered from head to toe—learned how to care for his bees and harvest the honey with a protective layer of smoke.

Our yard was also full of botanical lessons. My parents were both lovers of flowering plants and trees and had lined the perimeters of our property with alternating white dogwoods and showy, pink formosa azaleas. In the backyard, they'd planted a Granddaddy Gray Beard shrub and a Japanese Magnolia tree. They reserved a row or two in the garden for colorful zinnias and marigolds, grew morning glories up trellises, and cultivated white bearded irises in beds near the house. Each year, Mom cut a blooming iris and stuck it in a vase for us to experiment with in our kitchen laboratory. We added red, blue, or green food coloring to the water and watched the flower suck the color up into its petal's veins.

We carefully captured snakes and black widow spiders and dumped them into glass Mason jars so we could observe them for a little while. And when our cat gave birth to a litter of kittens, we observed that, too—up close and personal—with our faces right on the edge of the box screaming, "Here comes another head! It's a black one!"

A magnificent vegetable garden wrapped around the back and side of our yard. My parents grew peas, okra, cantaloupes, beans, turnips, potatoes, and more, and all of us hoed, pulled weeds, watered, and prayed for rain. One year, my dad erected fenced cages for his tomato plants. He babied those tomato plants and fed them a steady diet of Miracle-Gro until the plants produced hearty vines and mammoth tomatoes. Our neighbors marveled at my dad's tomato plants. With every visitor, he took the time to explain every detail of how he had grown the spectacular specimens of the tomato world and plucked a tomato to give to them as a parting gift.

I learned much from that yard and those experiences. I developed an appreciation and understanding of science and nature. It's where my deep love for all living creatures originates. It's where my fondness of flowers and gardening began.

That's where I came from.

My mother has always had a giving, angelic spirit about her. She smiled a lot and was a trusted friend to many—even hard-to-be-around people and folks who didn't reciprocate her kindness. She pampered my father, who was not the easiest person to live with, treated him like a king, and overlooked his many idiosyncrasies. She was an optimist who greeted most days with a cup of coffee and a hearty rendition of, "Oh, What a Beautiful Morning." She chauffeured my brother, sister, and me around town to the endless practices, meetings, and ball games, and she never once complained. Not once.

She believed in telling it like it was—even if the message was somewhat uncomfortable.

"You got my sorry hair, Amber," she often reminded me, lifting and examining sections of my long blonde hair and shaking her head. And when I was a teenager, she often said, "Looks like you aren't going to have any boobs. Your sister got all the boobs. You're going to be flat chested like me, or as your Grandmother Lanier says, 'flat as a flitter.'"

But those brutally honest, it-is-what-it-is remarks were counterbalanced with sporadic celebrations of my more positive attributes.

"You have a good head on your shoulders, honey," she said. "Be thankful for that. Not everyone is born with common sense and intelligence."

Mom was charged with keeping us girls in line. She delivered the "birds and the bees talk" to my older sister and me on four or five occasions. My sister, Audrey, and I shared a bedroom, and she always had a date lined up on the weekends. As she primped in our dresser's mirror, Mom would come in, flop down on one of the two twin sized beds in our room, and watch my sister apply her makeup and twist her pretty brunette hair around a Clairol curling iron.

"You know," she would start, "if either of you girls ever came home pregnant... that would be bad—very bad. I think I could accept it, but your father—he couldn't, and so you'd have to go live somewhere else. It would break my heart, but you'd have to go." And then Mom would get up and walk out of the room. It was more like a drive by shooting than a discussion about sex and relationships. The "talk" made quite an impression on me. I believed her and took her words literally.

I had a younger cousin in Macon who got pregnant out of wedlock when she was about sixteen. I was eighteen at the time and remember Mom telling me. I was mortified. Mom used it as a teachable moment saying, "Well, that's what happens when you play around and you're not married. I don't know what she will do now. She can't take care of herself, and she certainly won't be able to take care of a baby. It's sad, but she's on her own."

The baby came. And then another baby came not long after the first. Then another. My cousin lived in a rusted-out mobile home with a much older man who beat her. She brought four little girls into the world in just a few years.

On a few occasions when I was home for the weekend from college, I rode with Mom to Macon to a very old, disheveled trailer park in a seedy section of town and waited in the car as Mom took in sacks of groceries, diapers, and clothing and gave my cousin money. She talked to my cousin about options—about planning an escape and reclaiming her life. Mom returned to the car, and we drove home in silence. If she spoke at all, she would simply say, "Charity begins at home, Amber. Always love your family and take care of them when you can." Whenever my cousin's name came up in conversation, Mom talked about her with such love, compassion, concern, and anguish.

Mom gave my cousin and her predicament a lot of mental and physical attention, and as a young adult in my formative years, I was a bit confused. Mom's "talk" had led me to believe that there were good girls and bad girls in the world, and the bad girls were left to navigate this great big blue ball "on their own," so I didn't understand why she was wasting her time and energy trying to help my cousin.

I'm embarrassed to admit I felt that way, but I did. As an adult, I now realize that I misunderstood everything—that Mom's talk was merely an attempt to scare me and prompt me to choose abstinence instead of sex until I was at least thirty or forty years old. I now look back and admire what my mother did for my cousin, and with shame, I see so clearly how self-centered and callous my thoughts and frustrations were.

I came to realize my Mom was—and still is—a consummate advocate for the less-fortunate, the downtrodden, and the underdogs of our family, the community, and society. Whether they are struggling with alcohol addiction, poverty, abuse, horrendous family situations, or mental or physical disabilities, Mom was—and still is—always there to prop them up and love them.

When we were in Macon, we often visited a lonely, old man who lived a few doors down from the shop on Rocky Creek Road. His name was Mr. Stevens, and he didn't smell very good, and neither did his house. We'd visit for a while and Mom would make sure that he had bread and milk and that he was okay. He wasn't directly related to us. He was my uncle's wife's sister's father-in-law, and Mom decided he needed a guardian angel, and she assumed the role with no strings attached. She couldn't turn her back on someone who needed kindness and a hand up.

That's where I came from.

We took our newspapers and glass bottles to Happy Hour Workshop, a recycling work site for adults with developmental disabilities. When I was growing up, we used the word, "retarded" to describe the workers, who would help us get the newspapers out of our trunk and back seat. Mom turned on an extra dose of friendliness around the workers, making a point to speak to each one, smile, and thank them. As we drove away, Mom waved goodbye and said, "Oh, that's just the saddest thing, isn't it? They just want to be loved and help others. That's all. I'm glad there's a place like this, aren't you?" I nodded in agreement.

"Have you ever imagined what it would feel like to be retarded?" she'd ask. "Or the parents of a retarded child? If you are ever feeling sorry for yourself, Amber, just think about that for a few minutes."

Mom often put herself in other people's shoes to try to understand how those people felt. I saw her empathy and boundless kindness time and time again.

But along with that softness, she possessed a superhuman-like strength and fortitude that emerged during times of crisis. My mother is the quintessential steel magnolia.

My father died suddenly in 1992 when my mother was just 55 years old. In the hours after Daddy's shocking death and in the midst of crippling grief, Mom rose like a Phoenix, took charge, and began delegating tasks to each of us before the sun was even up that morning.

"Honey, sit down there at the table and let's make a list of everything we need to do and everyone we need to call," she said to me. "We're going to need to write the obituary this morning. The mall opens at 10, and we'll need to go and buy your father a nice shirt to be buried in."

I was numb and zombie-like, but her words forced me to focus beyond the death of my dad.

"When your sister gets here later today, we'll all need to go to the funeral home," she continued. "Later this morning, we need to call Bobby Simmons and talk to him about arranging a Masonic burial for Herman."

I nodded and scribbled the notes in a notebook Mom kept on the kitchen table.

And Mom even offered bits of humor in those painful days, to lighten the mood. At the funeral home, we toured the room where a dozen or more caskets were arranged like shiny cars with stickers listing features and prices of each.

"Wow! Your father would drop dead if he saw these prices," she whispered to my siblings and me.

She was our rock, and we leaned heavily upon her for comfort and healing—still do.

Mom was also a workhorse, a great cook, a gifted seamstress, a bowler, a beginner piano player, a devoted homemaker, a loving sibling to eight brothers and sisters, a sander of ceramics, a teacher of lessons, a friend that friends were lucky to have, a watcher of birds, a cunning detective, and an aspiring writer.

And I am my mother's daughter blessed with her strength and resilience; her patience; her smile; her brown eyes; her love of singing in the car; her desire to make everyone happy and keep the peace; her will to write stories, and most of all, her compassion for others.

That's where I came from.

At fifty, I understand more than ever that who I am is not only a function of my DNA—it is a function of the places where my body took root and grew and the experiences I witnessed, thought about, and learned from. It's a function of a small group of people who shaped my identity like I was a lump of clay on a potter's wheel.

Know my background, my family, and my stories, and know and understand me. It's that simple.

I am who I am because of where I came from.

Becoming History
By Marla Aycock

Growing up in the state of Michigan, *history* was never my cup of tea. I'd sit in a classroom at school staring out a window searching for a distraction. I'd create interesting patterns from dandruff on the boy's shirt in front of me to avoid the drone of names, dates, and deeds, of those long dead and gone. Looking back, I realize some of my disinterest was the dull manner in which it was taught. However, one U. S. History class in high school captivated me as the teacher brought stories to life with her narrative and theatrical reenactments. That one class was the only time my interest was sparked until my life gained its *own volume* of history. Then, my *history-buds* were piqued. Who were my ancestors, the people whose genetics and DNA influenced who I am?

Our youngest daughter, Esther, seemed to be born with a thirst for our family's history, and from a toddler begged to know stories of me and my husband's childhoods, and eventually that of our extended family. Once again this whet my appetite to know more of my personal background. Whatever family stories I'd neglected when Esther was younger, were revealed to her by my sister Lanette. Lanette, also loved history and had the old family picture albums, including treasured black and white *movies* of my maternal *great* grandparents—sweet morsels, for the history-starved, young Esther.

As in any family you'll find a mixture of the good, the bad, and the ugly when you sift through your personal genealogy and folklore. When the stories are positive, such as, "My uncle was the mayor of the city," we swell with pride to have such a prominent family member. The one word you don't particularly want to hear is *murderer*. The story of my great uncle is a mixture of *murder,* and strangely enough, *honor*.

My maternal grandmother, Emma Turner Tison, was raised in southern Illinois in a family of eight children; four girls and four boys. So I had many relatives with the last name of Turner.

One of Grandma Tison's brothers, my Great Uncle Harrison Turner, made the front page of The Daily Register in Harrisburg, Illinois on May 16, 1921. (We still have the newspaper clippings.) He married a woman named Lula who was incredibly beautiful.

We're talking *movie star* beautiful. To this day I'm captured by her beauty in the black and white photos we have of her. Lula started having an affair with a local man, making no attempt to hide the fact in this small town setting. She seemed to enjoy an *in-your-face* flaunting of the relationship as she brazenly rode through town with her lover, taunting her husband and bringing great shame to her family. This behavior extended over a long period of time. Finally, the ill-effect it was having on their ten-year-old daughter brought Harrison to the end of his emotional limits. He got his gun, drove to where her lover was and in front of witnesses shot him several times. He was dead at the scene.

It shook the town's moral fiber to its foundations, as such violence was rare, and Harrison was known as a man of sterling reputation. His wife's behavior must have been publically despicable and extremely onerous because on November 12, 1921, the jury returned a verdict of Not Guilty! To everyone's amazement, Lula and Harrison remained married and had a second child, a son, Harry Lee. Later a tragic mining accident claimed Harrison's life when he fell through a mine shaft, plummeting to his death 200 feet below.

Our family made the news again on July 17, 1923. The Daily Register of Harrisburg, Illinois ran a story about my Great Aunt Madeline Turner Reed and her family. Aunt Maddie was my Grandma Emma's sister. A rather juicy story was echoed through our family and was verbally shared with me from the time I was young. I guess you could say such family tales were the *soap operas* of their time. The story which circulated through the family was that my Great Uncle Robert Reed, his wife Madeline and their only son, nineteen-year-old Homer, had plans to move to California. Short on funds, the parents decided to burn down their home for insurance money to help them realize this dream. Plans were made for their nineteen-year-old son to be at a friend's home the night this event was to take place. Unknown to the couple, their son, Homer, unaware of the plot, changed his plans and was in his bedroom asleep when the dastardly deed was implemented. They became aware of his presence as they heard his screams from inside their burning home. Quoting from the newspaper article… "As Homer jumped out of his bed and dashed through the burning rooms and out of the window, he left a sad trail. The fireman reported...On the floor in the first room he entered was the skin from one of his feet. On the window through which he jumped was also found part of his flesh, torn probably from his back. On the ground directly under the window was found the entire skin from the other foot. In the grass where he fell after jumping through the window was a pool of blood, all of which tell the great pain and torture the young man went through. It is not sure he can survive the shock as he was burned practically all over his body." After about twelve hours of great suffering, he passed away at three-thirty that afternoon.

The newspaper article went on to report the words of the only witness of the events as follows... "Conductor Rufe Wells of the interurban, who was passing the Reed home at 3:55 o'clock, heard an explosion, which resembled noise that would follow when a light is touched to gasoline, rather in the order of a pop...Just as he neared the Reed home he saw flames in what he believed were the two rear rooms."

Whether the parents purposely set the fire was never proven and how it started according to the newspaper was a mystery. So whether the family created the spicier version of the story or it was just an unexplained tragedy we'll never know. (Hmm...Maybe this is why so many Turner families ended up in Michigan near us?)

Well, now I have the *bad* and the *ugly* revealed, let's look at one man in our lineage who redeems our tattered history a bit. My Maternal Great Grandfather E. L. Tison was an itinerant preacher. Each Sunday he rode on horseback to nearby rural towns to preach the gospel of Jesus Christ at rural churches where the congregations were without a regular pastor. When I heard his story growing up with my backdrop of 1960's stylish automobiles, travel via horseback seemed anciently cool.

Esther's beloved Aunt Lanette, moved to Washington D. C. during President Reagan's last year in office. Before there was an ancestry.com, genealogy became one of her passions as she now had access to both the National Archives and those at the Richmond Virginia Family History Center. As she dug deeper into our lineage she uncovered stories of our family history here in the U.S. dating back to mid-1600. To think we had ancestors who fought in the Revolutionary War was just crazy to my *history resistant* mind.

At one point Esther and I visited the National Archives with Lanette to see microfilmed histories of our forefathers. To personally look at national census records filled out in our own ancestors' handwriting was a stirring experience. They became more than a family story; they were real people. What a *shock* to find our *northern* family from Michigan had deep *southern* roots. They were primarily Virginians, with a few from Kentucky and Tennessee. The Virginians were even plantation owners with slaves. Distastefully shocking! A three time's great cousin designed the confederate flag. Are you kidding me? Our relatives who lived in Charlottesville, Va. lived near Thomas Jefferson and raced horses with him. Then we find we are distant cousins of General Lee. *"Wwwhaat?"* Again, this was a bit of impressive…but unsettling news to our northern mindsets.

From our Yankee perspective, *our* most *infamous* relation was a southern hero. The Reverend Ovid Kinsolving served the southern cause as a spy in the Civil War. He was the rector of Episcopal churches in border towns which changed hands dozens of times during the war, so he was ideally located to pass through Union and Confederate lines in his course of pastoral duties. Esther, a true southern belle, born in the south, was in family historical heaven as the discoveries came rolling in.

It seems the flame of a latent author's gene has fanned my soul as I enter the golden years of life as an aspiring author and find a connection to another southern relative, Barbara Kingsolver, an author of noteworthy fame. Okay, okay, I know, "Stop with the swelled head and the sullied pride to which I have no right, right?" Amidst all the family stories and discoveries of colorful southern fibers woven through my Yankee veins, many adjustments have been made in mind and attitude; I find *history* has become a *fascinating* subject.

ADVICE FOR ASPIRING WRITERS

We represent many types of writers. Newbies and established. Published and not-yet-published. Story tellers and tall-tale-tellers. From children's picture books to horror stories, stories about our past to stories about the future. From freelance articles to devotionals, poems to technical manuals. We have written for money, we have written for free, and we have written at a cost. But one thing we all have in common, we are writers!

So, what makes a writer? Having something to tell.

Maybe you, too, are a writer. Here in this section, we have composed some advice for those who want to write or who already write and wish to get better. Our hope is that you will feel inspired by our words to step out and share with the world what you have to say.... or at least share with those thoughts with us. We would love to hear them.

Good luck, fellow writer.

My Advice to Aspiring Writers
By Amber Lanier Nagle

Though I can't pinpoint the exact year the desire to become a writer sprouted from within me, I often look back at my history and realize I was destined from birth to travel the writer's path. Like an heir to some royal throne, I was fortunate to be born into a family of master Southern storytellers, and so, perhaps the writing gene is branded upon my DNA. Whether I was sitting on the front porch swing on a warm summer day, pushed up in a ladder-back chair to my grandmother's large farm table, or in the backseat of the car nestled between my older brother and sister, I was surrounded by raconteurs, and I listened, observed, and learned the art of storytelling from the best of the best.

I was also drawn to books, especially picture books with their whimsical words and illustrations. I loved the way books felt in my small hands and the intoxicating aroma of the pages. I remember skipping to my family's big, green Oldsmobile with an armful of picture books and a toothy smile painted across my freckled face. Reading good stories brought me so much joy.

When I was six or seven, my family became regular viewers of The Waltons, a television drama about a family's experiences during the Great Depression. From a bedroom on the second floor of the farmhouse, the narrator—John-Boy—wrote about life on Walton's Mountain at the beginning and end of each episode. I watched and listened to his words. I, like John-Boy Walton, wanted to preserve and share the stories of my family.

I'm not exaggerating when I say—I felt the earth move under my feet when I read To Kill a Mockingbird as a young adult. Like Harper Lee, I, too, wanted to share a powerful story with the world—a story that would be read by the masses, reveal hard truths, and precipitate discussions and perhaps, healing.

Yes, writing called to me several times through the years, but I never picked up my pen. I never tried. I always said, "Someday, I'll be a writer." That day came in 2001 when I was thirty-six years old.

The company I worked for declared bankruptcy and locked its doors overnight—a sudden and demoralizing experience for me and hundreds of my coworkers. The search for another job was slow and painful. I began to write to fill the void in my time, and because I found it somewhat therapeutic. I wrote three or four very short narratives about my childhood including a proverbial chicken story. I got up the nerve to send the stories to the editor of a nearby small-town newspaper, and he published them. A few weeks later, he asked me to write a column with similar pieces, and I agreed. Writing the column was more of a hobby than a job, but it forced me to sit down once a month, gather my thoughts, and compose something—anything. It was precisely the nudge I needed to develop my writer's voice and my own technique for storytelling and writing.

Ten years passed, and once again, I found myself on the threshold of losing another job. I took an online class for less than $100 and learned the secrets of selling my writing. Two months later, I sold my first article to Alabama Living Magazine. The check was small, but the satisfaction it gave me was enormous.

As of today, I've published hundreds of nonfiction articles in regional and national magazines and newspapers; I've published a paperback anthology titled, Project Keepsake; I've released two eBooks; I'm the editor of three regional magazines; I write a weekly column for a newspaper in South Georgia; I occasionally host writing and freelancing workshops; and I am working on a novel.

There are writers who have had greater commercial success than I have experienced, but I have learned much along my journey. Here are a few tips pulled from my lessons-learned file.

- Read. Read a lot. Read all sorts of material. And when you read a passage that sings to your soul, study it, dissect it, and try to determine what makes the writer's words or structure so powerful. Reading will ultimately make you a better writer.

- Write. Write a lot. Pick up your pen and put pen to paper (or fingers to keys) and write fearlessly. Carve time out of your busy schedule and write something. Write a love letter, a poem, a memo to your children, a shopping list, a blog, a ransom note, or an elaborate obituary for a family member. Like exercise, the act of writing will train your writing muscles, and over time, writing will become easier and easier.

- Resist the urge to edit—at first. Get your story down on paper first and edit later. Slowly read your story aloud and fix problems. Make sure your subjects and verbs agree. Check for consistent verb tense usage. Look at spelling, capitalization, punctuation, and grammar. Remove unnecessary words, sentences, and paragraphs. Construct smoother transition sentences and paragraphs. Think about the sequence of events in your story and consider moving paragraphs around to make the story flow better. After you edit your story, set it aside and let it simmer for a week or two. Move onto other things and try not to think about your story. Then pick it up and revise it again.

- Use bolder, more expressive verbs. Want to amp up your writing overnight? Find all the verbs in your sentences and where you can, replace boring, lackluster verbs with active, gripping, attention-grabbing verbs that pump life into your sentences and inject energy into your stories.

- Craft incredible hooks. First impressions matter, and in writing and storytelling, a writer only has a few seconds to impress a reader. That's why the hook is a critical component. The hook is the first sentence, the first paragraph, the first page, or the first part of a story or article that grabs—or hooks—the reader's attention and keeps him or her glued to your story. Study your first passages and work on them until they jump off the page. The Internet is full of tips to help writers improve their hooks. If you are still struggling with the beginning of your story, I suggest you pick up a copy of Ava's Man by Rick Bragg and read the prologue. Look at the way Olive Ann Burns started her classic Cold Sassy Tree. Read the first chapter of Janisse Ray's Ecology of a Cracker Childhood. Learn to develop a great hook from these storytelling geniuses.

- Find a tribe of writers and contribute. Ask for help from more experienced writers and offer assistance to those you can help. Attend writers groups and critique sessions and participate. Remember the Golden Rule of Writing, which is simply, "Do unto other writers as you would have them do unto you." Help others promote their books. Write book reviews for other writers. Attend their events. Be encouraging when another writer has temporarily lost his or her confidence. It's about reciprocity.

- Build as you go and celebrate each milestone along your journey. I started writing a monthly column—for free— about my family and my relationships for a small newspaper. Then, I wrote a few press releases for nonprofit organizations for a larger newspaper for a small fee. Next, I wrote a short nonfiction article for a small magazine, and after it was published, I wrote a longer nonfiction article for a medium-sized magazine. I kept building and building, and occasionally, I'd pat myself on the back and say, "Good work, Amber! Way to go! Keep going!" If you've never really written anything, it will be difficult to sit down one morning and peck out the next New York Times' Best Seller. Start with small projects and build to larger projects. Make progress and congratulate yourself from time to time.

- Backup your work every few days. This could be a writer's commandment—Thou shalt backup your work. A friend of mine recently lost several chapters of a book. Needless to say, he was devastated. Whether you backup your work on an external hard drive, save to the cloud, or save a second copy of your work every week on a thumb drive, make sure your work is protected.

- Always have a notebook handy, or keep another means of recording great ideas at your fingertips (smartphone, tablet, etc.). Why? Because when a great idea pops into your head, you want to be ready.

- Keep a few basic tools on your bookshelf. These items may vary, but here are five books I peruse often: 1) Simon & Schuster Handbook for Writers (for basic grammar and composition questions), 2) The Chicago Manual of Style (for more specific style questions), 3) The Writer's Market (to find paying markets for my writing), 4) Anne Lamott's Bird by Bird (for inspiration), and 5) Stephen King's On Writing (because I love it).

- Build a clip file. A clip is a writer's term for a writing sample. I have two active clip files. The first clip folder contains my own articles clipped from magazines and newspapers, in case a client wants to see examples of my articles in print form. The other clip file includes miscellaneous articles by other writers. These clips showcase interesting topics, clever hooks, or examples of beautiful writing I use to bring inspiration on days when my brain needs an extra boost or a fresh idea.

- Accept that writing is not easy. Expect your writing journey to be a somewhat difficult one with potholes and detours and delays. In episodes of Sex in the City, writer Carrie Bradshaw lights a cigarette, pours herself a glass of wine, and pecks out an interesting, well-written column in minutes before rushing out to meet Mr. Big at some exotic New York fine-dining establishment. I wish it was that easy, but it isn't. Some days, the words flow effortlessly and all is well with the universe, but on other days, the words don't come and you have to push them out like giving birth to an elephant. And stress often accompanies writing—especially when there is a deadline breathing down your neck. The sooner you accept that writing is not a cakewalk, the better.
- Don't be discouraged by rejection or failure. Just smile and know that it is part of the journey and all writers go through it. I often tell aspiring writers who attend my workshops that they will never hit a homerun if they don't step up to the plate and swing. If you fail at something (and you will), learn

the lessons from the experience, put the experience behind you, and move forward.

- Learn to say, "I'm a writer." Stand up tall, scoot your feet apart about two feet, throw your shoulders back, place your hands on your hips like a superhero and say, "Yes, I'm a writer!" Feel it. Believe it. And never be afraid to say it out loud.

Try Blogging
By Millicent Flake

Once upon a time writers toiled away in isolation, hunched over a typewriter or yellow legal pad. The only feedback they received was if they shared their work with a critique group or sent it to a publisher. Writing was a lonely endeavor.

Not so today. Now writers have many options for sharing their creations, including social media, online writers' groups, and blogging. Blogging is a great option for promoting books, finding others with similar interests, or sharing stories and journal entries.

Blogs, originally called 'weblogs', are websites in which authors post their work and receive immediate feedback and comments from their readers. Bloggers cover all subjects and are as diverse as the people who write them. Do you want to share your love of photography, painting, cooking, sewing, woodworking, gardening or running? Are you going through a difficult time, such as a divorce or cancer diagnosis and need to vent your thoughts and feelings? Are you a mother of young children or a child of aging parents and need to connect with others going through a similar experience? Do you have stories stashed away in a drawer that need to be shared? Then a blog may be for you.

Starting a blog is free and relatively easy. Wordpress is the most popular platform, but others used by our CAW members include Squarespace, wix.com and Blogspot. The initial setup may take some time and effort, but once that is done, posting is easy. Pictures and links to articles or websites can be added to make the blog more interesting and interactive.

Blogs allow for immediate feedback through "likes" and comments, which is encouraging and helpful to the writer. Readers can "follow" a blog and receive emails or a Facebook post when a new one comes out and some popular blogs can have thousands of followers.

A few years ago I started my blog of devotional thoughts, "Under the Magnolia Tree", and although I do not have thousands of followers, I have a small group of faithfuls. I have loved the comments, both private and public, that my readers send to me and the conversations with new and old friends on subjects that are often deep and personal have been the most rewarding part for me. And since writing is like any other skill and needs to be practiced, blogging helps me improve.

Karli Land, the founder of CAW, makes a great point about starting a blog: *There is nothing to lose in starting a blog. Worst case scenario, no one reads it but you get practice with your writing.*

So jump into the blogging world and share your stories! You never know where you will end up!

Start your Own Writers Group
By Karli Land

A writers group is important to the life of a writer. So what do you do if there isn't one meeting in your area? You start your own!

When I moved to Calhoun a few years ago I immediately began searching for writing groups that met in the area. I was shocked to discover that even though Gordon County was full of literary talent, a writers group was nowhere to be found. I felt a strong desire and determination to pull all of that talent into one room so that I could learn from those already playing in the big leagues. I have since discovered that the support and comradery of a writers group is absolutely irreplaceable. We naturally attract to people who share the same interests and ideals as we do. Belonging to a tribe provides a great sense of kinship. Fellow writers can provide understanding, encouragement, motivation and guidance that those who don't share the passion simply cannot offer.

As a participant of the Rome Area Writers, I was able to see the structure of a basic writers meeting. I am forever in debt to this group as it was their passion that drove me to start the Calhoun Area Writers. I would encourage you to start with another group, even if it means making a trip each month. This will allow you to learn about meeting itinerary and see what works. You can the take that information and tailor it to work in your area. My group meetings are much like what you will see in the Rome meetings and very much like what you would see in my Dalton group. We open with announcements which gives members an opportunity to share about upcoming events and also brag on recent successes. We then have a time of learning about our craft by way of a guest speaker. Through this, we have had the opportunity to meet many great authors and learn the ins and outs of the writing and publishing journey. We end our meetings with a time of sharing. Each member is given the opportunity to read some of their writing to the group for constructive feedback and encouragement.

We kicked off the Calhoun Area Writers with an author event in August 2014. I highly suggest having a big event to ensure a strong start . We invited several local authors to come speak about and sell their books. These local gems provided a ready-made following and were able to reach folks interested in writing through their already established networks. Events like these can be as elaborate or as simple as your time and budget will allow. Just be sure to have plenty of room for your authors to each set up a table to present their books. You may want to consider having a local bookstore host the event if that is an option. They are able to handle all book sales allowing authors to spend more time mingling with guests and signing books.

Now that you have a room full of potential members, show them what you have to offer. Be sure to have a full calendar of events planned to get your guests excited about coming back. Let them know what to expect at meetings and give them reasons to be apart of your group. Talk about the benefits of membership and how they can get involved.

And finally, who will your members be? So often I find writers who are timid about joining a writers group. They feel that if they could just improve their craft a little bit then they would be ready to seek membership. It is easy to fall prey to the belief that writers groups are filled with established and seasoned writers who have books on best seller lists. The reality is that there are probably more beginners than you think. A successful writers group will have a variety of members working together to hone and polish their skills. Aspiring writers can benefit from the learning that takes place in a group setting. They are able to connect with other beginners and share a bond as they journey together on their way to publication. A more established writer can provide mentoring that can help other members tremendously. And, in reality, the publishing industry is ever-changing and there is always something new to learn, regardless of prior accomplishments.

Now, it's time to get planning!

If you ever have questions or need advice, I'm only an email away.

-Karli Land
karlilandwrites@gmail.com

In The Company of Georgia Writers
By Amber Lanier Nagle

There must be something in the water in Georgia that grows master writers and storytellers. Mistress of many deep, folksy short stories, Flannery O'Connor was born in Savannah before moving to Andalusia Farm, just outside of Milledgeville. Sidney Lanier was born in Macon and went on to compose nationally celebrated poems like "The Marshes of Glynn" and "Song of the Chattahoochee." Coweta County boasts writing greats Erskine Caldwell and Lewis Grizzard. Margaret Mitchell pecked out the Pulitzer-Prize winning novel Gone with the Wind from her apartment on Peachtree Street in Atlanta. The luminous Olive Ann Burns created a setting for her epic, Cold Sassy Tree, based on her hometown of Commerce. Writer and folklorist Joel Chandler Harris grew up in Eatonton, as did Alice Walker who wrote The Color Purple. Pat Conroy was born in our state's capital. Georgia's poet laureate and acclaimed novelist Judson Mitcham was born in Monroe.

The last several decades have witnessed a tsunami of Georgia writers crashing onto the literary scene, climbing the bestseller lists, and chalking up prestigious awards and honors. We asked a few Georgia authors to tell us about their writing journeys and offer a few tips. Here's what they said.

TERRY KAY (terrykay.com)
Born in Royston, Georgia. Writes from Athens.

Terry Kay says he never intended to be a writer. He graduated with a Social Science degree from LaGrange College in 1959 and got married.

"My goal back then was to make money and provide for my family—that's all," he says.

He landed a job as an errand boy for the Decatur-DeKalb News and found himself surrounded by writers, journalists, and stories. He learned the trade of reporting and moved to The Atlanta Journal in 1962.

"I gradually learned what was required to be a writer," Kay says. "It's not something you learn overnight."

Though his first novel was published in 1976, Kay's signature novel, To Dance With the White Dog, wasn't released until 1990. It quickly took its place of honor among Southern literary classics, was made into a Hallmark Hall of Fame, made-for-television movie, and established Kay as one of the South's most beloved writers.

Today, with seventeen books to his credit, Kay is working on a play and a novel set during WWII.

"I don't write to tell a story—I write to discover the story," he says.

Tips from Terry Kay:

Rewrite everything. It doesn't really start taking shape until the third draft.

Find a good writer, with good material, and sit down and copy his or her work word for word. Something will happen during that exercise—some type of spiritual osmosis. When you finish, you'll be a better writer.

Don't overwrite. Trust the reader with adding what you have left out.

SALLY KILPATRICK (sallykilpatrick.com)
Born in West Tennessee. Writes from Marietta.

Sally Kilpatrick wrote her first stories in elementary school.

"Each week, my fifth grade teacher had us write a story that included all the week's spelling words," she says. "We had to get really creative to use all twenty words."

She graduated, went to the University of Tennessee, and earned an English degree. She married, moved to Georgia, taught high school Spanish for eight years, and gave birth to two children. She enrolled in a professional writer's program at Kennesaw State University.

As her life unfolded, she always carved out time from her busy schedule to pursue her writing and in 2010, she completed the first draft of The Happy Hour Choir.

"The publishing world moves slowly," she says. "But I kept writing throughout the process."

In 2013, she didn't just sell one book to Kensington—she sold three and optioned a fourth. Her books fit nicely in the Southern fiction genre, featuring quirky, familiar characters navigating through the maze of life's unexpected events.

"I'm working on the fourth one now. It's titled Bless Her Heart," she says.

Tips from Sally Kilpatrick:
Finish the book you are working on and keep writing. "If I had stopped writing after I finished my first, I would have only sold one book to my publisher," she says.
Set writing goals that are attainable and within your control.

RAYMOND ATKINS (raymondlatkins.com)
Born in Massachusetts. Writes from Rome.

Ray Atkins moved to the South when he was thirteen. "I've been observing the people here for a long time," he says. "I think most writers are observers of people."

He was first published around 1978 in a college literary journal.

"But then I took a thirty year break from writing to get married and have children," he says. "I had to pay bills, so I worked as an Industrial Maintenance Manager."

His first novel, The Front Porch Prophet, was published in 2008 and was awarded the Georgia Author of the Year Award for First Novel. Since then, he's published four more novels and is working on another titled, Set List. He's the "English guy" at Georgia Northwestern Technical College and is a staff member at Rhinehart College's MFA Creative Writing program.

"I write books that help people get through the day," he says. "Life can be hard sometimes, and I like to offer hope. I love the promise of some type of redemption."

Tips from Ray Atkins:
Sit down, write, and get your story on paper.
Write the truest thing you know.
Make writing the first thing you do every day.

JANISSE RAY (janisseray.weebly.com)
Born in Baxley. Writes from Altamaha.

Janisse Ray's father tossed the television out of the house when she was a toddler.

"So I was raised surrounded by the stories of real people, my relatives and the townspeople around me," she says. "…my father believed that poets belonged up in some exalted place alongside the saints, so I was encouraged to write, and I knew from a young age that I wanted to be a writer."

She studied creative writing at college and graduate school. She published her first book, Ecology of a Cracker Childhood, in 1999 when she was thirty-seven. The book was showered with awards and accolades and was featured in the New York Times.

In 2015, Ray took her rightful place in the Georgia Writers Hall of Fame. She's working on her seventh book.

"I write to help alleviate suffering—human and otherwise," she says. "To save those things worth saving. To educate. To awaken people to the power of love."

Tips from Janisse Ray:
Be nice and learn to fall in love with people. Listen to them. They will tell you their stories, and this is the biggest gift they can give you.

KARIN GILLESPIE (karingillespie.net)
Born in the Minnesota. Writes from Augusta.

Karin Gillespie finished her first novel when she was thirty-eight but erased her manuscript from her hard drive after attending a writer's conference. However, she had attended a session titled, "Southern Fiction is a Hot-Seller," and was so inspired that she went back to her hotel room and started a humorous Southern novel that would later become Bet Your Bottom Dollar.

"A slew of editors rejected it, but one had some interest if I agreed to do some revisions that would make it into a series," she says. "Naturally, I said yes. Later my agent called me and offered me a three-book deal with Simon & Schuster, and of course I said, 'yes,' to that, after screaming a little."

Today, she is the author of the Bottom Dollar Girl series, Girl Meets Class, and the upcoming Love Literary Style. She is also Georgia Author of the Year in the romance category.

"[Writing] has taught me that it is perfectly fine not to know what my next step will be," she says. "But if I keep going and trusting, all will be be revealed."

Tips from Karin Gillespie:
Keep moving. Write the book, then start the next one.
Read The Anatomy of Story: 22 Steps to Becoming a Master Storyteller by John Truby. "I recommend it to anyone writing a screenplay, a short story, or a novel," Gillespie says.

LYNN CULLEN (lynncullen.com)
Born in Indiana. Writes from Atlanta.

When she was five, Lynn Cullen wrote her first story about a bear that ate so much honey, he had to roll home in a barrel.

"So, I knew I wanted to be a writer from a very young age," she says.

She studied English Literature at Indiana University and took writing classes at Georgia State University. While raising three daughters and working part-time to help with family finances, Cullen began working on a middle grade novel. The Backyard Ghost was released seven years later when Cullen was thirty-five.

"Twenty years and fifteen children's books later, my first adult novel, The Creation of Eve, about the student of Michelangelo and first female painter, Sofonisba Anguissola, was released," she says. "I had to get the kids out of the house and teach myself how to write historical novels—with all of the arduous research that goes along with it—before I could publish the type of literature I was born to do."

Today, Cullen award-winning, bestselling novels have been picked by NPR, People Magazine, Target, and even Oprah. Mrs. Poe is currently under development with a film production company.

"But my favorite honor is to have novels on the Books All Georgians Should Read list, as Twain's End currently is."
Tips from Lynn Cullen:
Be willing to learn and believe in yourself.
Dig as deeply as you can into telling a truth about the human condition. Go for that almost unbearable truth.

A Selection of Georgia Writer Museums, Memorials, and Landmarks

Georgia Writers Hall of Fame (University of Georgia)—recognizes Georgia writers, past and present, whose work reflects the character of the state—its land and people. Learn more or browns the honorees at georgiawritershalloffame.org.
Margaret Mitchell House (Atlanta)—Birthplace of Margaret Mitchell's Gone with the Wind with an assortment of interesting

photos, writings, and objects. Learn more at atlantahistorycenter.com/mmh.

Sidney Lanier Cottage (Macon)—birthplace of noted poet, musician, and soldier, Sidney Lanier (1842-1881). Browse Lanier's flutes (a silver, alto flute made by the Badger Flute Company), Mary Day's wedding dress of 1867, and several portraits and first editions. Learn more at sidneylaniercottage.org.

Lewis Grizzard Museum (Moreland)—A collection of Grizzard's typewriters, family photos, mementos and manuscripts are on display.

The Little Manse - Erskine Caldwell Museum (Moreland)—The museum includes books, movie art, U.S. and foreign versions of Caldwell's work and a video presentation.

Andalusia Farm - Home of Flannery O'Connor (Milledgeville)—A 21-acre farm complex where Flannery O'Connor and her mother lived and where the author wrote all her published work. Read more at andalusiafarm.org.

Flannery O'Connor Childhood Home (Savannah)—A museum houses restored to its Depression-era glory with guided tours that reveal the quiet domestic life of the young Mary Flannery and her family. Read more at flanneryoconnorhome.org.

The Smith-McCullers House Museum (Columbus)—Childhood home of Carson McCullers. Read more at mccullerscenter.org/museum.php.

Dream a Little Dream
By Elizabeth Amonett

On my thirteenth birthday, I received a baby blue lock-and-key diary. I thought it was beautiful. The crisp, blue-lined paper was edged in gold and protected by a soft cover and a little gold clasp. It smelled fresh and new, but I sprayed Love's Baby Soft Perfume on it to make it smell sweet. I had found myself a trusted friend and from that day forward, I started a lifetime habit of journaling.

Soon afterwards, I sat in the backseat of my pastor and his wife's car on my way to church youth camp. My long hair flying all around my face and in my mouth did not deter me. It wasn't enough to just write things down. I needed to tell someone! I babbled nonstop about the extensive journal entries I had written since my birthday.

In one breath, I explained:

"Since I was six years old, I knew I was going to be a music teacher, just like Mrs. Olson, I just love and idolize her. Well, as the years went by, my dream flourished. I have plans. I'm going to study hard, go to college, meet my Christian husband, get married, teach music, live in a large white ranch-style house with glossy black shutters, raise horses, and depending on the state of the world, I will have zero to four children, but there is a serious derailment to my future plans! I broke up with Steve last night. He wanted to hold my hand, and I'm not ready."

I was knee deep in explanation when my pastor's eyebrow arched in the rearview mirror. "Elizabeth," he said, "keeping a diary is a good thing. Most young girls write only about their upsets and heartache, so please… remember to write about your happy thoughts, too."

Over the past four decades, I've tried my best to adhere to my pastor's wise advice.

While in school, my beloved music teacher, Mrs. Olson, nurtured my love for music, teaching dreams, and God-given talent for twelve years, from first grade until my senior year of high school. During that last year, she helped me secure a small vocal scholarship to Evangel College, a Christian liberal arts school in Springfield, Missouri.

When I graduated high school, I could have flown to Evangel College on pure excitement. My childhood dreams were finally coming true. Two days after arriving there, I watched my family drive away in our 1972 Oldsmobile and fear sprouted in my heart. The first tears of doubt streaked my face.

During the four months between that sad August moment and late December of 1979, my excitement vanished and my lifelong dreams evaporated. Growing up in my little hometown, I had been a big singing fish, but then suddenly, it felt like I had jumped from a familiar pond and was drowning in an ocean filled with extremely talented musicians.

I was a ballad girl. To this day, I still long for sweet, tender melodies and well-written lyrics. But at Evangel? I sang what I was told to sing, and I could barely read music! Mrs. Olson, family and friends had told me I had a lovely voice, but being a soloist in a sea full of performers wasn't good enough. When I could no longer hold my head above water, my lifelong vision of teaching music sank, and it took all my accompanying hopes and dreams with it.

Should I quit school? Change majors? Maybe I could be a folk singer? You know, forget all the technical stuff, just sing and play guitar. Nope. With a soprano voice, they had me singing opera-style vocals and insisted that if I was going to be a music major, I had to master sight-reading.

Overwhelming confusion had replaced my dreams. Insecurity became the cherry on top of the mounting homesickness and disillusionment. I finally gave up. Daddy was easy to convince. He never wanted me to leave in the first place. Mom, however, had worked hard to get me to Evangel and me fulfilling my dream was her dream. She was so proud of me and spoke about sticktoitiveness. I shattered her dream when she found out I had quit Evangel without her consent, but with the condition I stay in college, both parents dutifully received me back home.

From that life-changing decision, I then bumbled and stumbled in a wilderness of higher education and jobs. I set goals and accomplished them. I devoured what seemed like thousands of textbooks and wrote what must have been millions of school assignments. I changed majors three times. As I bounced along, I met my husband and, together, we built a marriage. Life expanded and I grew comfortable.

It took only ten years to earn my four-year business degree. By the time I finished school, I was already established in a career in the business world. I was happily tap-dancing my way through life and had settled into a steady and easy flowing rhythm.

Although my dream of becoming a music teacher had died years ago, my love for every genre of music still lived. Throughout all life's floundering, I managed to keep a song tucked inside my heart. I sang in church, but mostly I sang in my car and shower. I wrote song lyrics about subjects that touched my heart and expressed my faith. Because I had some understanding of music theory, I taught myself to play a few chords on the guitar and piano and had an instrumental background for my words. If there was any acknowledgement of creativity on my part, it was always in reference to music.

By the time I was forty, however, I had developed a lifetime of writing habits, journaling, school assignments, business letters, personal notes, letters and short stories, and songwriting.

Then, my marriage crumbled.

I wrote my husband a nine-page letter in a desperate attempt to communicate where spoken words had failed. One year later we divorced. To keep my sanity, I wrote and wrote and wrote.

For the first time in my life, raw, vulnerable emotions spilled violently onto the page. I worked hard with my creative writing skills in order to express deeply personal issues in a cryptic way. It was challenging to write honestly without sounding like a high school drama queen and blatantly baring my soul on paper for others to possibly see.

During the healing process, I also emailed inspirational 'thoughts for the day' to my family and friends, which I now realize were mostly self-imposed therapy sessions.

Then my mother died.

My ninety-four-year-old grandmother was unable to visit or attend the memorial service. With my heart in the right place, I wrote Grandma a tender and lengthy letter sharing intimate details of Mother's last days.

Because the letter contained priceless memories, I sent copies to my sisters. One sister shared it with her friend who suggested I turn the long letter into a book. Those words flattered me. I had written for decades, but since I had lost my two main confidants in life, my husband and my mother, I had been journaling more than ever to express myself, and the book idea brought a new perspective to my writing habits. Why not? So just like that, a new dream was born.

I now have a burning passion to compose stories and publish them. This wonderous *art* of writing has moved into my heart and shares space with the beautiful art of music and it has created in me a new vision for the second half of my life.

This new dream differs from my childhood dream. I've learned from life. For starters, my confidence does not rest in others opinions, nor does it rest in my own understanding and knowledge, or my abilities, or my gifts and talents. I know that without the Lord, I can do nothing. But with God, all things are possible.

In addition, I better understand how dreams fuel passion, and while passion can give birth to our longings, it is only an emotion and it rises and falls like every other feeling. In the beginning, dreaming is easy. Enjoying its rewards is also easy, but enduring the entire course of a dream takes more than strong passion, it requires perseverance. A vision must be planted in the rich soil of a firm commitment and then fertilized with prayer, time, and hard work. When commitment and hard work meet a God-given opportunity, it is harvest time, and we will bear much fruit.

The dream I am committed to and work long hours to develop is to become an author. The story that brings me the most joy in writing is the historical fiction book about my ancestor, Jacob Amonett. He was a French Huguenot who fled France in 1685 due to religious persecution. Huguenots were protestants. Jacob escaped death and lived in Holland and England for several years before coming to Virginia in 1701. Jacob is my six-times great-grandfather.

I have been writing the story of Jacob Amonett for several years. I joined the Calhoun Area Writer's (CAW) group in July 2014 when Karli Land, our founder, held its first meeting.

Since joining the group, my skills have advanced and I've learned more about the craft of writing. But more than this, I have become part of a unique and priceless group of writer friends. As each relationship deepens, the fictional story of Jacob Amonett blossoms and other story ideas have also unfolded, including a series of historical novels written with Christian themes based on eight generations of descendants from the Jacob Amonett line.

I have been writing all my life, but only recently have I begun to call myself a writer, so my best tip for writers is this: Do not be afraid to dream a little dream.

If you have a passion to tell a story or say something to the world, I encourage you to take time and write it. A God-given dream will burn deep in your soul and will birth an uncompromised knowing.

My goal now is to complete the Jacob Amonett novel and have it published. As I move toward accomplishing this dream, rewards fall all around me. I have sold magazine articles, grown as a writer and as a person, and I've made new friends.

In summary, I ask you to please keep your eyes and ears open for my novel, "A Sacred Journey, the Amonett Family Book One" when it is finally published. I hope you will be one of the first to buy this suspenseful, historical family drama of how Jacob escaped death and moved to America. Your support will be greatly appreciated.

With a sincere and grateful heart, I thank you for taking the time to read these thoughts. I also want to extend one final word of encouragement to you, "Commit to the Lord whatever you do, and He will establish your plans" (Proverbs 16:3NIV).

Inspiration
By Vickie McEntire

All writers have periods where they lack inspiration. When I find myself in such a place, I read...and listen. A very wise writer I know, Paul Moses, once said, "Writing without reading is like shoplifting in an empty store."

Reading how other writers write, can inspire you to incorporate something about their style into your own writing. You can learn something from every book you read, and your writing style becomes a beautiful patchwork quilt influenced by all your beloved authors. Authors who have inspired me are Sean Dietrich, Jimmy Carter, Elizabeth Gilbert, and Malcolm Gladwell. Certain books you will learn to keep at your fingertips, because when you read just a short piece of your favorite writer's words, you can be instantly transported to a state of inspiration.

I follow Sean Dietrich on Facebook, and every morning while I'm having my coffee, I read his latest post. His stories are based on true circumstances that have happened in various southern locations. After reading some of them, I find my coffee has been sprinkled with tears. I am so inspired by his style of writing, that I have tried to imitate it in my own writing in my story, "Red, White, and Blue", in this anthology.

Jimmy Carter is the author of twenty-nine books. This man was the thirty-ninth president of the United States and was awarded the Nobel Peace Prize in 2002. Yet he still found the time, and felt it was important, to write about his hometown in his book, *An Hour Before Daylight: Memories of a Rural Boyhood.* His southern drawl can be heard in the words on every page, and it inspires me to tell my own story.

In her book, *Big Magic Creative Living Beyond Fear,* published by Penguin Random House, Elizabeth Gilbert writes this about inspiration, "Most of my writing life consists of nothing more than unglamorous, disciplined labor. I sit at my desk and I work like a farmer, and that's how it gets done. Most of it is not fairy dust in the least. But sometimes it *is* fairy dust. Sometimes, when I'm in the midst of writing, I feel like I am suddenly walking on one of those moving sidewalks that you find in a big airport terminal; I still have a long slog to my gate, and my baggage is still heavy, but I can feel myself being gently propelled by some exterior force. Something is carrying me along—something powerful and generous—and that something is decidedly not *me*." I was so inspired by her words, that I started my next novel on one of the blank pages in the back of the book!

I like to read Malcolm Gladwell, because he takes complicated data, looks at the big picture, drills down into the tiniest moments, and helps explain why things are the way they are. That's the way I understand his writing. It's inspirational to me, because he can take a complex topic and make it very understandable to the lay person, which is me. His writing reminds me to write with my own voice, and strive to make the story easy to comprehend for all readers.

When I pick up a new book and spend two days straight reading it, because I can't put it down, I always look back and wonder *how did that author do that?* Any time you read an article or story that flows so seamlessly that you forget you are reading, look back at it and try to understand why.

Reading blogs by other writers can be another useful way to find inspiration. I enjoy reading several bloggers. At cheryllsnow.com, I'm inspired by timeless stories that make me laugh and cry, and laugh again. Millicent Flake inspires me with her southern style in her blog, *Under the Magnolia Tree*. A fun blog by Karli Land, *Karli's LaLaLand,* provides humor, whimsy, poetry and a sweet story about her Memaw. Amber Lanier Nagle, specializing in memoir writing, gives a marvelous tour of family life in the south. Ginger Anderson weaves her wonderful sense of humor into everything she writes on her blog, *Ginger's Grocery*. All of these blogs offer inspiration and specific writing tips, too.

We don't just want to hold an audience captive, we want to have something important to say, and that is where inspiration comes in. If you're experiencing writer's block, step away from the empty page. Go out into the sunshine, and let nature take your mind off the business of writing. Once you relax, inspiration floats down upon you like soft snowflakes on the frozen ground. Sometimes, just driving to work or watering my garden gets my mind quieted enough to hear the stories stir within me that want to be told. One of my favorite quotes from Kahlil Gibran's *The Prophet* reminds me of the big picture, "You are the bows from which your children as living arrows are sent forth. The archer sees the mark upon the path of the infinite, and He bends you with His might that His arrows may go swift and far. Let your bending in the archer's hand be for gladness; for even as He loves the arrow that flies, so He loves also the bow that is stable." One might replace the word "children" with "creations" to understand how writers feel about their work.

Some folks would suggest a beautiful writing journal for capturing your inspired thoughts, but I say use whatever is available when inspiration hits: a paper napkin, little tiny sticky notes, the back of a receipt, the palm of your hand, or record it on your phone's voice recorder. It probably is a good idea to carry a small notepad around with you, but the lack of one should not keep you from writing down those inspired thoughts.

Listen up. If you hear someone say something that you feel is profound, write it down. If it keeps calling out to you, then explore your own perspective about the topic, and write about it. I like to listen to most genres of music. It's interesting how an old song can trigger a memory and a wellspring of emotion. I would take that recollection as a signal. Follow the guidepost and find your inspiration waiting.

Attend writers' conferences. I met Georgia Author of the Year, Victoria Wilcox, at The Writers Forum in Rome, Georgia, which is a conference hosted by the Rome Area Writers. Ms. Wilcox was inspired by a house she frequently drove past while running errands. She used that inspiration to write her trilogy of books, *Southern Son: The Saga of Doc Holliday*. The first time she saw the house it spoke to her. Every time she drove past it, the house called out to her. She listened. Now, she inspires other writers.

Sign up to have online forums delivered direct to you via social media. Two that I follow are Suite T—The Author's Blog of Southern Writers Magazine, and Writers Write. These will not only further your understanding of the craft of writing, but may also be a source of inspiration by those out in front leading the way.

Last, but certainly not least, join a writing group. You might enjoy reading *The DOs and DON'Ts of Writing Critique Groups* by Amber Lanier Nagle on her website ambernagle.com. The Calhoun Area Writers group has motivated me and energized my writing to a level I had not imagined possible. I am inspired by the members of our group every time we get together. You've seen just a glimpse of their talent on the pages of this book. Hopefully, you will find inspiration on these pages as well.